Julie Hornok knows how to draw readers in, capture their hearts, and leave them inspired. I have had the privilege of publishing Julie's work in the autism community for many years and have witnessed the incredible difference her articles and blogs have made in the lives of thousands of families in more than 180 countries. Julie writes with a depth of honesty and passion that is hard to come by.

—KENT POTTER
Founder and CEO of AutismSpot

United in Autism: Finding Strength inside the Spectrum offers a look into the lives of families around the globe sharing the experience of living with autism. Julie Hornok does an incredible job of curating the real-life stories of these fascinating children and their parents, and this book will undoubtedly open the eyes and hearts of all who read it.

—WENDY FOURNIER
President of the National Autism Association

United in Autism

United in Autism

Finding Strength inside the Spectrum

Julie Hornok

BROWN BOOKS
PUBLISHING GROUP

United in Autism
Finding Strength inside the Spectrum

Brown Books Publishing Group
16250 Knoll Trail Drive, Suite 205
Dallas, Texas 75248
www.BrownBooks.com
(972) 381-0009

A New Era in Publishing®

Names: Hornok, Julie.
Title: United in autism : finding strength inside the spectrum / Julie Hornok.
Description: Dallas, Texas : Brown Books Publishing Group, [2018]
Identifiers: ISBN 9781612542737
Subjects: LCSH: Parents of autistic children--Anecdotes. | Autism in children--
    Anecdotes. | LCGFT: Anecdotes.
Classification: LCC RJ506.A9 H67 2018 | DDC 618.92/85882/02--dc23

ISBN 978-1-61254-273-7
LCCN 2018937719

Printed in the United States
10 9 8 7 6 5 4 3 2 1

For more information or to contact the author, please go to
www.JulieHornok.com.

To every parent who has heard the life-changing words "Your child has autism." Together, we are stronger.

Contents

Foreword

Dr. Temple Grandin

As I read through the stories written by mothers and fathers who have had a young child diagnosed with autism, I see that many at first felt devastated and lost. They did not know which way to turn. Their feelings are normal. When parents call me, I always recommend that they join a local parent support group. Parents will know where the best services are located. Autism varies greatly in severity. When I was three, I looked completely terrible, with no speech, rocking, tantrums, and other autistic behavior. Fortunately, many hours of speech therapy and playing turn-taking games helped me to become fully verbal. My ability in art was always encouraged. When children are two to five years old, it is difficult to determine which ones will become fully verbal and which ones may remain nonverbal and have other medical problems along with autism.

There is a great variation in the quality of services in different states. Some states have excellent educational programs, and others do not. All children with autism benefit from therapy. The worst thing that can be done with a young child with autism is to wait and do nothing. If you are in an area where educational services are poor and private therapy would be too expensive, do not despair. Many people have put together their own successful programs by getting volunteers from their church or community group to work with their young child. Screen time must be severely limited. These kids need to interact with people. There are some books I would recommend to parents who have to develop their own program, including:

- *Autism Breakthrough* by Raun K. Kaufman
- *Uniquely Human: A Different Way of Seeing Autism* by Barry M. Prizant
- *The Way I See It* by Temple Grandin

Acknowledgments

To my husband, Greg: thank you for believing in me and supporting me in ways no one else could. I love you!

To Lizzie: your hard work, determination, and ability to adapt to the world continue to inspire me. I am blessed to be your mom.

To my favorite sons, Andrew and Noah: thank you for making your own meals when I was busy writing and understanding how long "ten more minutes" really meant.

To my mom, Marilyn Statler: thank you for always being "the wind beneath my wings." I could not have written this without your editing and support.

To my mentor, author Jackie Waldman: your heart is gold. I am honored to know you and eternally grateful for your guidance and encouragement.

To my sister, Katie Bangert, for helping with the nitpicky details of query and proposal writing. I was only able to hit "send" because I knew you had looked over it.

To Kristin Rankin and Danielle McCormick for listening and praying me through every step of this project.

To Carrianne Photography and Pala Photography for the beautiful pictures.

To the rest of my family: your prayers and support in this project have been felt. I love that I actually *like* my family!

To the most brilliant MAFEA autism moms, who gave me guidance and support in those grueling early years of autism. Your wisdom helped me put the pieces of Lizzie together, and your friendship kept me from feeling isolated.

To the autism moms on the National Autism Association of North Texas board. Not only do you give your time, knowledge, and experience to the community, you have fun doing it. You motivate me to continue to fight the good fight.

To all the friends who helped me find these thirty families across the globe, thank you for sharing your connections.

To the thirty parents who shared your stories with me, thank you for showing others what strength within the journey looks like. I am so grateful for your vulnerability and for allowing me into your world. You are truly an inspiration!

To the Brown Books Publishing and Agency at Brown Books teams: thank you for taking on this project and believing in the impact it will make.

To Temple Grandin: by sharing your wisdom openly with the world, you have helped me understand and support my daughter to help her become the best version of herself. Thank you from the bottom of my heart for your support of this project.

Introduction

Like most afternoons, Lizzie, my daughter with autism, and I had decided to take a walk to the park. This afternoon was different because our normally quiet, calm sanctuary had been taken over by a large, loud family event. Little kids were running around, chasing each other and flying kites; the older kids were playing basketball. All the adults were congregated in the center of the park, sitting in folding chairs near the tables of food. The scent of hamburgers on the grill filled the air with energy and anticipation.

I thought the crowd might be too much for four-year-old Lizzie, but she walked right up to the adults and stood there observing the scene. I was so excited she seemed interested in the people. They began talking to her. "Hi there. What is your name?" No response from Lizzie. "Wow. You sure are cute. You have the most beautiful brown eyes. How old are you?" they continued to ask. I began answering for her since I knew she would not. As we chatted for a while longer, Lizzie walked among their smiling, happy faces and made herself at home. She even hopped up on one of the empty chairs and happily swung her feet while quoting the words from her favorite movie.

Normally, Lizzie avoided being near people, even her family. She was happiest when playing alone in her room. So when Lizzie put herself in the middle of this festive, fun group, my hopes for her future began to rise. *Maybe she really is capable of relationships. Maybe if we are a little more fun at our house, Lizzie will show more interest in us.*

"Lizzie, it is time to go home," I said. "Tell the nice people goodbye."

She looked toward the group of adults and said, "Goodbye, tables. Goodbye, chairs."

The entire time I had been chatting with the people to support Lizzie's interest in them, Lizzie had actually been more interested in the wide array of tables and chairs!

Yep, that's autism in a nutshell.

As we walked away hand in hand, I started laughing. I must have looked crazy, but I knew if I didn't laugh now, the second I got home, I would never stop crying.

Autism can be a lonely journey. Just when you think a big step of progress has been made, another challenge rears its ugly head. After interviewing thirty autism parents around the world, I realized each of them has felt every emotion I have felt, from hearing the crushing words, "Your child has autism," to longing to hear my daughter tell me, "I love you." I truly have more in common and feel more connected with autism moms living thousands of miles away than I do with someone living right next door.

Lizzie was always a little different. I remember watching her in her crib when she was days old and feeling she was looking through me, not at me. She was an easy baby, which I appreciated since I also had a busy toddler demanding much of my time. At six months, she was still engaged with us but would sit on the floor and page through books for hours. When she learned to crawl, she would giggle as her older brother made a game of chasing her around the room.

Then, one day, she stopped noticing the world around her. She would crawl superfast and slam into the wall. We originally thought this was hilarious, but back then we had no idea of the rabbit hole she was about to go down. The diarrhea, the rashes, the fevers, the ear infections, the permanent snotty nose, the night sweats, the night waking, the screaming in pain, the banging her head on the ground, the lining random things up, the opening and closing of cabinet doors, the high-pitched screams, the tantrums, the loss of language, the refusal to answer to her name, the flapping of her arms, and finally the complete isolation from everyone who loved her. She was diagnosed just after her second birthday with moderate autism.

Although I was devastated, getting Lizzie back became my full-time job. We began an in-home, thirty-hour-a-week program with speech, OT (occupational therapy), ABA (applied behavior analysis), and Floortime. We put Lizzie on a strict gluten-free, dairy-free diet and slowly tackled all her other physical health issues. Little by little, month by month, she made progress. She started using her words to get what she wanted almost right away, and by six years old, she was beginning to form the ability to have short conversations. With hours of therapy and consistent help in school and at home, she continued to progress. As she progressed, we backed off the help and let her fly.

Lizzie is the hardest working, most disciplined girl I know. She has a loud, positive energy that sucks you in and makes you want to be a part of her world. At fourteen years old, she is fully mainstreamed, has friendships, is a cheerleader at school, has a paid job, and actively participates in our world in every way a typical child would. But she still has autism. She has this watered-down, beautiful version of autism that displays childlike innocence coupled with wise determination. She is quirky and fun and different. She brings to our world an out-of-the-box perspective we would be foolish not to learn from.

Somewhere along the way, I began to share the therapies that worked for Lizzie with others. I didn't want what I had gone through to be wasted. My heartache meant something if I could now help others with more vulnerability than I was capable of before autism. I joined the National Autism Association of North Texas Board and began a successful yearly event to pamper moms of kids with autism. I also started a blog to share autism's humorous side and created a website to show Lizzie's progress through videos.

I can't wait for you to meet these extraordinary parents who have risen above autism's tough circumstances to use what they have learned to help others. Each one has felt the suffocating isolation autism often brings and has come out of that aloneness by seeking out other autism parents. By joining with others, these parents are able to give back to the world, impacting the lives of so many in a positive way. The peace in this journey comes from accepting we are all working together as a part of a bigger plan.

Nagla Moussa

Plano, Texas, United States of America

Alvin, Twenty-Nine Years Old

If there had been eerie music to build suspense, it could easily have been a scene out of a horror movie. Even though the odd display under my feet was a daily occurrence, it still sent chills up my spine every time I turned the corner into the hall leading to the bedrooms in our home.

On this particular day, I was in a hurry, so there was no one to blame but myself. I had been doing laundry all morning. Maybe it was a selfish desire to feel the satisfaction of a completed job or simply a reassurance that I was still capable of keeping my home organized and flowing like it did before everything happened with my son. All I wanted was to feel a sense of normalcy.

We should have left five minutes before, but I had one last load to fold before I whisked my son with autism, Alvin, off to therapy for the afternoon. I was looking forward to sitting peacefully in the waiting room knowing the clothes were clean and dinner was in the Crock-Pot. Maybe I would even pull out a new research book on how to heal the gut and find a gem that might improve his condition.

As I hurried around the corner toward the bedrooms, the large laundry basket in my arms blocked my view of the hall floor. My toes hit something hard, and I felt the figures scatter beneath my feet. "Oh no!" I wailed. I knew this meant we would not be able to leave home for another hour. Therapy would have to wait.

Alvin was obsessed with Pokémon. He had every figure ever made, which meant there were hundreds of them "decorating" various rooms in our home. These figures were one of the few things bringing him joy, so we indulged him. But with the pure, childlike happiness he displayed as he received each new one, there was a dark side. He loved to line them up. He spent hours fixing their arms and legs exactly how he wanted them, then lined them up from his bedroom through the hall to the bathroom. It still creeped me out when I turned the corner and saw all those beady little eyes staring back at me. I'd learned my lesson not to touch or move these figures even an inch, or a massive meltdown lasting for hours would ensue. The only way to manage this obsession was to allow him to meticulously put them back in place. There was no changing his mind; this was the way it was.

Alvin was four years old when he was diagnosed with autism. For two years, we had known something was different about him. He would lie on his back watching the fans spinning on the ceiling. He never came when we called his name, had no eye contact, stared into space, and repeatedly bounced Matchbox cars against the wall. Autism was not common in 1990, so it took a long time to get a diagnosis. When we did, my then-husband was working full time and going to school, so Alvin's care was up to me.

We began therapy and started him on a medication, which caused him to regress even further. After much research, I learned how diet and vitamin and mineral supplementation could help him physically and mentally. We replaced the medication with natural treatments, and Alvin began responding to therapy and regained some language. Although progress was slow, we were moving in the right direction.

In 1995, a teen with autism, Michael Clemons, was shot and killed by a police officer while his parents were out of town in the suburb where I live. Michael was nonverbal and did not respond to the commands given by the officer. This news devastated me. I could not help but think this could have been my son. The intentions of people with autism are often misunderstood. This tragedy highlighted the fact that our police officers desperately needed education in how to identify and help those living with autism.

Together with Michael Clemons's parents, I lobbied to pass legislation requiring police officers to have training on developmental disabilities. We trained these officers ourselves, and a beautiful relationship of continued dialogue began with our city's finest. I loved the feeling of being able to use what I was going through with my son to help others. It felt good to do something positive and see the changes happening right before my eyes. I wanted to do more. No, I needed to do more.

I joined a local autism organization and volunteered so much I was asked to be the president of the chapter. Eventually, our group became a chapter of the National Autism Association. Currently, we offer educational seminars for those living with autism, autism professionals, teachers, and staff. We plan fun events for families with autism and give autism moms a fabulous day of pampering. We have weekly support groups and self-advocacy groups and give grants to those in need of autism treatments, swim lessons, iPads, advocacy, and so much more. I love being able to give back. Sometimes, the more we give, the more we get in return.

My son is now twenty-nine years old and has progressed beautifully. He is a college graduate, has friends, and drives himself to work every day. He is kind, honest, and hardworking. With him, there is no guessing; he says exactly what he means. Being in his presence is restful for me, and he is my very favorite person to be around. He has changed so much from the days of staring at the ceiling fan and lining up figures. When I ask him now why he was so rigid about lining them up, he simply says, "My brain told me to do it and would not stop until I did." He still refuses to get rid of all those Pokémon figures, but thankfully, they are in a box somewhere in our attic . . . placed in exactly the right spot by my son.

The National Autism Association of North Texas
NAA-NT.org

Amanda Robinson

Pollington, East Riding of Yorkshire, England
Logan, Eight Years Old

I walked down the produce aisle at the supermarket, speedily weaving in and out of other peoples' carts as if I were in a high-speed chase on the motorway. I'd come well prepared with a list in hand and swiftly grabbed everything I needed to feed my family for the next week. I knew my son, Logan, was a ticking time bomb, and I hoped we could make it out the door before the explosion went off.

I was inches away from the checkout lane when the massive melt-down began. He went from zero to one hundred in fewer than thirty seconds; there was no stopping him once he began. He was screaming at the top of his lungs and flailing his arms in a full-blown tantrum. I quickly assessed my situation: if I left now, I would have to go through this all over again. No, it was best to ignore the tantrum and get through the checkout as fast as possible.

Just as I was about to lay my first item on the counter, a lady walked up to me, angrily waving her finger at my son, and said, "That child needs a good slap!" I stood there for a moment, stunned as her words pierced my heart. I had no quick-witted comeback or angry retort. I was humiliated. I grabbed my son, abandoned my cart, and ran to my car. The moment Logan was back in his seat, he calmed down. Now it was my turn to let it all out. I sobbed for thirty minutes before regaining enough composure to make the drive home.

It was nearly impossible to leave the house with Logan. His anxiety was so high and his behavior so out of control that we stopped going out unless completely necessary. Unfortunately, one of the necessary places was the supermarket. I only wished this was something "a good slap" could fix.

Logan's birth was traumatic. He was born four weeks early and deprived of oxygen for a short time. I have an older child, and as Logan grew, I knew I shouldn't compare, but Logan seemed to be developing differently than his sister. By six months, he didn't have eye contact and wasn't reaching his milestones. My instinct told me something was wrong, but every time I took him to the practitioner, I was told my son was a late developer.

Logan walked on tiptoe and was very rigid about how he played. Soon his moods were off the scale. The doctor told me to try time-outs. Before long, I was running back to the doctor every week looking for answers. I knew this was more than bad behavior. When Logan was two years old, I demanded help because he was not talking. We started speech and language therapy, but that wasn't enough.

Logan's meltdowns became more intense. He was so obsessive about how he had to do everything; it took us an hour to make the five-minute walk to school. I begged our general practitioner for some testing. He formed a social communications panel, consisting of a speech/language therapist, a pediatrician, and a psychologist. I filled out lots of paperwork and answered loads of questions. Each specialist came to my house to do an evaluation, and it took them nine months to finally come up with the result: autism.

The psychologist had mentioned autism to me during a visit, so by the time I received the formal diagnosis, I had done some research at the library and was expecting it. I had heard of autism but never needed to know or understand what it was. Now I did.

Logan was moved to a special school, but the school fought us for all the services we needed since Logan behaved differently at school than he did at home. They didn't realize he saved up the unhappiness and anxiety he experienced all day at school and fell apart when he came home. He was like a simmering teapot blowing his top the moment he walked in our front door. No one wanted to be around us, and who could blame them?

Living in a small village, we felt very misunderstood and isolated. No one believed what we were saying about our son's behavior. No one listened to what was really going on in our home as we struggled to find help. First the doctors and then the school treated us as if we were exaggerating his behavior. Why would we make up what was happening with Logan? Didn't they know we would give anything to have a normal life?!

At one point, Logan was so unhappy, he said he didn't want to live anymore. Such moments break my heart, but I have to grieve quietly without him knowing.

Logan began to progress when we got Rufus, our autism therapy dog, from Autism Life Dogs. Having a friend who required nothing of him was life-changing for Logan. Rufus gives him unconditional love, helps him burn nervous energy, reduces his anxiety, lays on him to calm him, sleeps with him, doesn't judge him, and helps him not feel so alone. Logan cares for Rufus daily and has been given a new purpose in life.

If I ask Logan to go out of the house, the anxiety sets in, and we may never make it past the front door. But if Rufus needs a walk, he happily gets dressed, brushes his teeth, and takes him out. Logan loves Rufus so much he will do whatever it takes to make sure he is getting his needs met.

After seeing such a difference in Logan with a therapy dog, I began training dogs for Autism Life Dogs. I love it! Training a new dog, knowing I can give this gift to another child who desperately needs a friend, is the best thing in the world! It gives Logan another purpose, too. He helps me with the dogs, and we meet the families when they come to pick up the dogs. These families become fast friends, because there is something about this journey we are on together that instantly bonds us.

Logan has a good life now. I tell him often, "Be yourself. Don't hold things in. You may have autism, but autism doesn't have you."

Autism has changed me too. I am braver, stronger, and have developed much thicker skin. The next time someone says something unkind to us at the supermarket, I will be ready with a snappy comeback that shows my son I love him exactly as he is. Society needs to change, not our kids.

Autism Life Dogs
AutismLifeDogs.com

Pam Minelli

Jupiter, Florida, United States of America

Andrew, Nineteen Years Old

The number-one killer of children with autism is drowning. As I ran down the street toward the beach, barefoot and screaming Andrew's name like a wild woman, I was terrified my eight-year-old son was about to become a statistic.

I loved living in our Florida beach community. The sun was always shining, and the warm breeze rolling off the water brought a salty smell that made me feel alive. My son had elopement issues, so our house was like Hotel California . . . You could check out any time you like, but you could never leave! Because Andrew had no understanding of danger, we had multiple deadbolts and extra safety precautions installed to keep him from escaping our home.

Contractors had been working in the yard all morning, and by afternoon, they were out of mulch. They had hopped in their truck to buy more, leaving the back gate wide open. The perfect autism storm was brewing. Our dog had pushed the back screen door open, making an easy way out for someone looking to explore beyond the safety of our home. And Andrew was always looking to explore.

Andrew loved the beach. A giant smile would come across his lips as he ran full speed into the water, splashing his hands against the waves. He was drawn to the middle of the ocean as if a siren were calling his name. He would swim farther and farther out until it was so unsafe my husband and I were forced to use our bodies as a blockade to redirect him back toward the shore. I worried about him getting so far out he would be pulled under by a riptide. Despite the challenges, the beach was our happy place . . . a place where even in the throes of autism, we could feel like a family.

The house suddenly seemed way too still. Andrew was a noisy boy—always humming and making quacking sounds—so when the house was quiet, we knew he was into something he shouldn't be. I ran to each room, expecting to find him opening the cabinets or making a mess with craft supplies, but he was nowhere to be found. My heart beat faster with each empty room, and then my eyes glanced toward the screen door . . . then the gate . . . and my heart sank.

"Andrew!" I screamed as I rushed out the door, knowing he would not answer to his name. "Has anyone seen Andrew?" I frantically asked the neighbors.

I sprinted toward the beach, where I knew he would be, the hot pavement burning the soles of my feet as I ran. The police were called. We all began to search. Finally, I heard the words that made everything all right again. "I found him! He's OK!" a neighbor yelled.

Andrew was standing on the beach, fully clothed and soaking wet. He had gone for a swim and decided on his own to turn back to the beach instead of swimming to the middle of the ocean. I was so relieved and grateful; my happy, smiley, cuddly, super affectionate son was safely in my arms!

At six months old, Andrew couldn't sit up. He was a chubby baby, so we didn't think much about it. But at nine months, he still wasn't sitting up, so we had him evaluated. We started physical therapy right away, and then it became obvious we needed to add occupational and speech therapy. The doctors were convinced he didn't have autism because he had good eye contact, and back then, it wasn't autism if there was good eye contact.

At two years old, he still wasn't progressing as hoped, so we tried chelation, behavioral therapy, listening therapy, and more. We placed him in a private Montessori school, but he only lasted three weeks.

When Andrew turned three, we went to a neurologist and pushed for a diagnosis. We knew it was autism and wanted to get him the proper schooling. With that diagnosis in hand, we were able to enroll him in a charter school specifically for children with autism.

Even though this school was tailored to kids with autism, it was not a perfect fit for my son. At one of our team meetings, his teacher told me, "Andrew said he enjoyed our circle time today."

"Well, that's nice," I responded, "but Andrew is nonverbal." She had him confused with another student. If they weren't even sure which child my son was, I knew we could do better.

We needed a school that had smaller classes, more personal attention, and innovative thinking. My son loved and responded to music; I knew he could learn this way. We found a wonderful school called the Learning Center where the classes were smaller, the learning was more tailored, and the teachers creatively used the kids' interests to teach them. I helped with fundraising and volunteered at the school so much they asked me to become the board president.

The Learning Center went only through middle school, so we raised enough money to open a high school called the Learning Academy. Later, our campus added early childhood and adult services.

Pro golfer Ernie Els moved to our area and placed his son with autism in the school. Els and his wife founded the Els Center of Excellence, and our lower and upper schools were soon delighted to be under the

Els Center of Excellence umbrella. I became the director of development for the Els for Autism Foundation.

I love using what I have learned to help build a community. Sometimes I think no one would believe the things happening in my home, but when I tell other autism families, I realize they are going through the same things in their own homes. It is so important to not feel alone.

Being able to help others by combining the skills I used in the corporate world with the knowledge I have gained from my son is more gratifying than anything I have ever done. I love being a part of something bigger than myself.

My son is now nineteen, and we are working on an adult housing center. We are building a safe community our kids with autism can be a part of, even when their parents are no longer living. My hope is this blueprint will be multiplied all over the world.

Els for Autism Foundation
ElsForAutism.org

Rahel Abayneh

Addis Ababa, Ethiopia

Nathan, Ten Years Old

Just as she always did, Kedist woke up early in the morning before the sun rose. Her son was still sleeping peacefully next to her as she slipped out of bed and quietly fixed his favorite breakfast, *kinche*, an oatmeal-like dish. Not wanting to wake him, Kedist lightly set the dish where he could easily reach it when the sun shone through the sticks that made up her home. She gently took the long ropes fastened to the bed, placed them around his wrists, tied the knots tight enough that he could not get away, gave him a soft kiss on the forehead, and walked out the door to go to work for the day.

In Ethiopia, children with autism are not allowed to go to school or join the others in childcare. It is a common belief that a child with a disability is a curse on the mother. Many times when a handicapped child is born, the dad's family will come to the house, tell the mom she is a disgrace to the family, and take the dad away to find him a new wife.

For Kedist, this meant that she, a single mother, would have to work long hours walking from house to house to find menial housekeeping jobs. Her son had no language, did not respond to commands, had no ability to care for himself, and had no awareness of danger. The only way to keep him safe was to tie him up while she was gone and pray that he would still be there when she arrived back home after dark.

Women like Kedist were the reason I could not flee my homeland to get help for my own son. God had given me a vision.

My son, Nathan, was not like my other two children. He did not socialize, did not talk, and had severe constipation. When I expressed my concerns, the doctor told me he was fine. But when my youngest passed two-year-old Nathan in skills, I took Nathan to a neurologist who did an EEG and diagnosed him with autism. We were told this was a lifelong condition with no cure and no hope.

The devastation hit hard. I could not eat for three days. I wanted to die. I prayed continuously for God to take me. I was so angry . . . Why had God done this to me? No one else I knew had a child with his condition. I mourned for two months.

Depressed, I began watching a TV network through our satellite dish that suggested taking a child with autism off of milk might help. I withheld milk and began giving Nathan enemas to ease his constipation. We saw progress, and within a few months, he was even potty trained.

My husband not only stayed with us but became our head researcher. We found therapies on the internet and began implementing them in our home. More progress. My husband found one school in all of Ethiopia for kids with autism. We made a phone call and were elated they would see us. We left Nathan with family and headed in our car to the school. Our hopes were high as we turned down the long road leading to the school on the top of the hill to register our son. The school was like an oasis in a barren land—a beautiful two-story home with several classroom additions in the back and a large playground in the front. The children playing were active and looked happy. I knew Nathan would get better once we got him in the school.

When we walked into the waiting room, it was a different picture all together. There were over thirty parents in the room; all looked sad and overwhelmed, and many were crying. Some had traveled over twelve hours by car. All of them thought they were coming to register their child for the school, and all of them, including us, were sent home without services. I went to the lady in the office and demanded to know why they would not accept my son. She pointed to the waiting list. He was number 463.

I began talking to the parents in the waiting room. One man had lost his wife to mental illness when his child was diagnosed. He had been coming to register his daughter for five years and now was told she was too old to go to the school. There were kids with horrible injuries from hurting themselves, and many poor, single moms looked like they were starving. I asked for phone numbers from those who had phones so we could keep in touch.

When we got home, I started meeting other families with autism. One neighbor had a boy they thought was allergic to the sun, but he actually had autism. I began teaching parents the things I did with my son that were helping. Soon they saw progress too.

Our family had connections and found several places for my son to get treatment in other countries. Even though I wanted to get him help, I couldn't go. God had already given me a vision. I was to build a school for kids with autism, especially the ones with no money. I would give others the tools to care for their child and return the hope they lost on the day of diagnosis.

We had many struggles finding the right funding and turning down investors who wanted to make this a for-profit business. We prayed and prayed. Finally, a priest gave us the money, and we were able to get a license. Soon God blessed us with more money than we needed to start building. By radio and word of mouth, families began coming to us with their children with autism.

One of the first to bring her son to our school was Kedist. She no longer needs to tie her son to the bed because he has a place to learn, grow, and be loved. He is learning to care for himself and can now put on his own clothes.

We started the school with six kids, and it grew to forty. Now we have over three hundred on our waiting list. I don't want to turn kids away. My vision is for not only my child with autism but all the children of Ethiopia to heal. We are working to educate and change the view of autism here. We are expanding to other locations, hopefully one in each region, so every child will be given the chance at a good life.

Nehemiah Autism Center
Nehemiah-Autism.org

Vonda Powell

Liberty, Missouri, United States of America

Austin, Sixteen Years Old, and Adam, Fifteen Years Old

The rain was pounding so hard on my windshield I couldn't see ten feet in front of me. "Not today," I groaned. "I can't be late!" Today was the start of my new career, and I wanted to make a good first impression. At twenty-two years old, my heart had been torn between my passion for music and the need to put food on the table. So I made the decision to give up my dream of singing on Broadway in New York City to live a "normal" family life in Missouri. I felt at peace with my choice as I walked through the school doors to pursue teaching music therapy to kids with special needs.

Butterflies began fluttering in my stomach when I was escorted to meet my first client, a nine-year-old boy with autism. He was a skinny little guy, jumping up and down, flapping his arms, bug eyed with anticipation. I knelt down so we were eye to eye, and just as the thunder clapped loudly in the background, I said, "Hi there!" He was nonverbal, and I am not sure if it was the thunder or if he couldn't politely respond to my greeting, but he lunged toward me and bit me as hard as he could on my arm. His strong bite broke through my fancy "first day of work" patchwork leather jacket, through the thick, green sweater underneath, and through my skin, drawing blood.

Immediately, the administration was called, a report was filed, and I was sent to a clinic for a series of shots. There was no way for me to know then that this was my first encounter with the developmental disorder that would define my life, my work . . . and my own two children.

My firstborn, Austin, was a typically developing baby. He hit all his milestones the first year. At fourteen months, he stopped talking, stopped walking, and began to scream ten hours a day. My youngest, Adam, had been born fewer than two months before, so I was drowning trying to care for a newborn and a toddler showing the angst of a teenage boy.

I dove into the alphabet soup of therapies for autism. We tried everything . . . diet, natural treatments, supplements, occupational therapy, speech therapy, behavioral therapy, hippotherapy, joining therapy, and so much more.

Soon Adam began to show the same signs. He was different, but he lacked language and connection in the same way, so by the time he was fourteen months, I knew he also had autism. My heart broke. Both my boys were struggling so greatly. When a new behavior arose, I would call my mom to ask if this behavior was me, them, normal, or autism. I had no reference point to know how a typically developing child acted. "Mom, I feel like I am sliding down a rope with my boys. I can't get ahead," I confided.

She responded, "Then tie a knot in the rope, and move forward one inch at a time."

It wasn't long before I found myself a single parent, desperately needing to connect with others living the same life. I initiated a playgroup for kids with autism through our early childhood services. We shared our resources and cherished the friendships that reminded us we were not on this journey alone. I began to mentor other parents and helped with events put on by numerous area autism groups. Giving to others enabled me to function. This was the driving force helping me stay positive and be a better mom to my boys. I had more energy and out-of-the-box thinking when I was helping others. I also loved the idea of bringing together the autism community to focus on how we could all work in sync toward our goal of bettering our kids.

Before long, I was known as the "go-to" in the community for special-needs resources and soon began a job as an autism specialist

/ family resource person. This enabled me to spread knowledge and training in disabilities on a much wider scale all across the state. My proudest accomplishments were being able to spearhead training four thousand first responders; employees at Worlds of Fun amusement park in Kansas City; and, most recently, the Kansas City Royals baseball team—from ticket takers to vendors, concession workers, and more—in autism awareness and acceptance. Families with autism are now able to experience a baseball game with their child in an autism-friendly environment.

Austin is sixteen years old and makes me laugh every day. He comes up with creative names for people and has a loving concern for others. Adam is fifteen years old and is like a giant teddy bear. He is nonverbal, but that does not mean he is nonthinking. He types to communicate with us, and it feels wonderful to finally know what is going on inside his head.

My life did not follow my plans. God's plans were bigger and better than anything I could have imagined. Although I didn't end up with a "normal" family life, this is my life, and I am so grateful my struggles have allowed me to help others.

Autism Outreach Fellowship Missouri
Facebook.com/AustimOutreachFellowship

Corinne Long

Budapest, Hungary

Grant, Eight and a Half Years Old

Photo Credit: Lauren Pupillo

As I stood by the mirror in my bathroom putting my makeup on, I was startled by my son, Grant, screaming with rage. "Why did you wake me up? I'm mad at you!"

I hadn't woken him up, but that was beside the point, because when Grant woke up in a "mood," there was no reasoning with him. Every morning when I got out of bed, I didn't know which Grant I was getting that day.

I'd made the mistake of allowing him to stay up late last night, and even though he knew we were taking Daddy to the Budapest Airport this morning, that was not on his agenda. "I am not going!" he wailed.

"Grant, we need to get dressed. Do you want to wear the blue shorts or the red shorts?" I asked patiently.

"No shorts!" he shouted. We somehow got him dressed and coaxed him into our blue station wagon, knowing the entire thirty-minute ride would be one unhappy comment after another.

My husband, Jonathan, pulled up to the curb of the airport, opened the door, popped the trunk, and began taking his suitcase out of the car. All five of us climbed out of the car, and one by one, we gave Daddy goodbye hugs. We would miss our "glue"—the strong man who held our family together. As I hugged my husband goodbye, he whispered in my ear, "I am sorry you have to do this alone. I will be back in three days."

I whispered back, "I will be OK. This is just a normal day." I kissed him hard and forced a smile.

Grant was still angry, so he stood there in protest, stiff, with his head down. Jonathan hugged him and told him he loved him, but there was no response from Grant. As he began walking to the check-in line, everyone but Grant smiled, waved, and blew kisses until he was out of sight. I started the car, hiding the tears filling my eyes as we pulled away. Jonathan and I were an exceptional team. I didn't want to do this alone . . . even if it was only for three days.

The world is a busy place. We are so preoccupied with our own lives that rarely do we slow down to notice the pain behind the smiles in people around us. To others, we may look like the picture-perfect family, but in reality, many days we are struggling to survive.

Grant, for the most part, was a normal baby. He spit up incessantly but hit all his milestones at the tail end of normal. As he grew, the spitting up turned into gagging and vomiting. His speech did not develop, and he repeated "lidle-lidle-lidle" gibberish all day long.

A speech pathologist friend came to visit and noticed Grant also walked on his toes. I had never noticed that before. She recommended we get him checked out for neurological issues. We took him to our pediatrician and then to a neurologist, and both came to the same conclusion: "He's perfectly fine! He's a boy. He will talk. Wait until four or five years. There's no problem." But I knew there was a problem.

We went to another doctor, who agreed there was something not right. This was the first time I heard the words "autism spectrum" connected to my son. I didn't know how this was possible since Grant was so social. Everything I knew about autism pointed to an introverted child who didn't like being around others.

Grant was also diagnosed with sensory processing disorder, low muscle tone, large motor skill delays, and speech and eating issues. We began an early-intervention program through the local schools, in which he received occupational therapy, speech therapy, behavioral

therapy, and physical therapy. Having Grant involved in so many therapies was overwhelming. Each therapist gave us strategies to work on with him at home, since the best progress is seen when the therapies are implemented in daily life. Working from home and having two other children to care for made it difficult.

Children in Hungary are seen but not heard, probably because when it was under Communist rule, people were afraid to speak out loud. The first time I went to a playground, I wondered where all the loud, boisterous children were. Children were playing quietly. Requiring a child to be quiet in public does not work when he has autism. I always have to be on alert. In every situation, I have my "Grant radar" on. I've learned to pick up the signals he puts out indicating whether he is emotionally stable or whether he is escalating into a meltdown. I need to be ready to intervene whenever necessary. It can be very tiring, and I am only relaxed when the kids are sound asleep.

My husband and I came to Budapest to do mission work. Grant's diagnosis has made me all the more passionate about serving the underprivileged in society, whether they struggle with disability, poverty, being an ethnic minority, or some other problem. As we work with Middle Eastern refugees or the castaway gypsy youth, I am constantly connecting their humanity with my own. I see the mother struggling to help her child. I see the abandoned youth no one else sees potential in. I see my own challenges and struggles reflected in the people we serve.

Grant has stretched me as a mom and as a human being. He has changed the way I parent my other children and taught me grace and mercy. Grant has refocused my priorities and taught me to never give up, while letting go of the need to be perfect. He is now eight and a half (the half is stressed by him). He is incredibly loving, always makes us laugh, is honest to a fault, and often says things that can be slightly embarrassing to us or to other people. We love him for who he is, no matter how many heads may turn in the quiet streets of Budapest when he laughs out loud!

One Mission Hungary
Hungary.OMS.life

Kirk Smith

Los Angeles, California, United States of America

JJ, Eighteen Years Old

Comedy brings people together to laugh. It takes the sting out of whatever is going on in our lives and helps us feel we are not alone. I do stand-up comedy all over the world. Talking about the funny things my son does helps me and others to realize that no matter what we are going through in our lives, if this idiot (me) can do it, they can too!

My son, JJ, is eighteen years old, is quite tall, weighs over 230 pounds, and is very strong. When he gets angry, he tears things. Mostly,

the "things" he tears are his clothes. This complements nicely with his love of being naked.

JJ has tactile issues, so his clothes must be loose fitting, tagless, and very soft. When he does wear clothes, he likes to wear pajama bottoms and will never, ever wear underwear. It may look strange to see an eighteen-year-old out in the world in his flannels, but clothing is the least of our worries. So as long as his private parts are covered, we consider that a green light to leave the house.

One day, we were running errands, and JJ decided he wanted ice cream. We are always trying to help him eat healthier, so I nicely told him no, and then we walked into the dry cleaners. As I was handing the man our clothes to be cleaned, I heard some all-too-familiar sounds behind me. I turned around to see that my man-child had ripped all his clothes off and was standing there in the waiting room completely stark naked. One less pair of pants got cleaned that day.

JJ was a beautiful, normal baby until he was about one and a half years old. He stopped answering to his name, walked on tiptoe, lost his language, flapped his arms, and would sit in a corner all by himself for hours with a blank look on his face. We thought he was deaf because he wouldn't answer to his name. We took him to the doctor to check his hearing, and instead, the doctor told us, "Your son has autism."

I had never heard of autism. I had to look it up, and what I found was basically what you see in the movie *Rain Man* . . . a genius boy with

lots of special gifts. We kept waiting for JJ's special skill to show itself, and we found out his skill was . . . nothing. Well, maybe being naked, if that is a considered a skill.

This was a super hard time for me. I was very athletic. I'd played basketball all four years in college, and I'd had hopes of going pro. Subconsciously, I had dreams for my kids, so when I realized my son would never play basketball, that I could never share this with him, it was difficult to take in. It took me a very long time to figure out his dreams are not my dreams. He was not missing out in life because he was not living out my fantasy.

We put JJ in a special-needs class for autism at our local school. It was real work to get him the services he needed. The system seemed to be set up to wear us down. We were mentally, physically, and emotionally exhausted, and we needed help. We had to think outside of the box to survive.

All we could do was take one day at a time, do the best we could, and then move on to the next day. Autism is like a bully beating the snot out of you every single day. The biggest thing is to find a way to not feel alone.

I put together a free podcast called *Autastic Podcastic*. Anytime someone is feeling down, they can put this on, laugh a little, and realize they are not alone in their struggles. Being honest and talking about what makes us uncomfortable is healing.

It is healing to give back to others. I grew up in a family of missionaries, and you will find most people who are happy are the ones who are also giving back. Focusing on someone else makes you realize there are people in the world who have it a lot worse than you do.

JJ now has about ten words and repeats language in context. He still struggles greatly. He is a big fan of food, though usually in unusual combinations. One of his favorite foods inspired the title of my account of life with JJ: *Rice Krispies with Ketchup*. "It does sound weird but tastes ok," I explain in the book. "It is not a snack you would think to try, but it is not terrible. It is the metaphor for our life. Our lives are not what we imagined they would be, they are different: not terrible, just very different, like Rice Krispies with ketchup."[1] All I can do is surrender to God . . . like it says in the serenity prayer.

Serenity Prayer
by Reinhold Niebuhr
God grant me the serenity
to accept the things I cannot change;
courage to change the things I can;
and wisdom to know the difference.

Living one day at a time;
enjoying one moment at a time;

accepting hardships as the pathway to peace;
taking, as He did, this sinful world
as it is, not as I would have it;
trusting that He will make all things right
if I surrender to His Will;
that I may be reasonably happy in this life
and supremely happy with Him
forever in the next.
Amen.

Even with all the difficulties, I still find ways to be joyful. In *Rice Krispies with Ketchup*, I reflect, "There are some positives to focus on. I don't worry about empty-nest syndrome; at this rate, the nest will never be empty. Also, I don't have to save for college. The biggest hurdle to him getting into college is not money; it's nudity."[2]

Ecuador Project Hope

EcuadorProjectHope.com

Autastic Podcastic
iTunes.Apple.com/us/podcast/autastic-
a-comedians-guide -to-autism/id984750988?mt=2

---

1. Kirk Smith, *Rice Krispies with Ketchup* (Kirk Nathaniel, 2013), 105.
2. Ibid., 110.

Denise Wetzel

Moscow, Idaho, United States of America

Mark, Sixteen Years Old, and Joshua, Thirteen Years Old

A mother's love is a complicated entity. Before having children, I had no idea I was capable of experiencing so many feelings within such a short time. One minute I am brimming with pride for the small steps of progress my sons have made, and the next, I am overwhelmed with frustration they can't do more. Never was I more aware of this swinging pendulum of emotions than the day my eldest son attacked me and ended up handcuffed in a police car.

It was a beautiful spring day in Idaho, which meant the temperature was above twenty degrees and the sun was shining. My sons, Mark and Joshua, and I bundled up and headed out for our Sunday walk. We lived close to a scenic, paved, one-mile trail along a creek, and the sound of the trickling water calmed and energized us. Every week, I cherished this special time with my boys.

Sixteen-year-old Mark was often frustrated, but he had never been aggressive before, so when he began grunting at Joshua, I calmly sent Joshua home. Joshua was often a trigger for "the Hulk" in Mark to come out, but the situation was usually easily diffused. As Mark and I continued to walk our normal route, his irritation escalated. He began demanding, "Cheeseballs! Cheeseballs! Cheeseballs!" When I told him we would need to go home for the cheeseballs, he hit me. Stunned, I stepped back. He hit me again. Then my six-foot-one, 230-pound son used the full force of his weight to lunge toward me with the intention of biting me. I managed to escape and ran behind a tree. After a few deep breaths, Mark seemed to calm down, and I felt confident we could safely return home.

We got only a few yards down the trail before he attacked me again. This time he was grunting and screaming in a rage. Between blows, I called 911. A man whom I recognized as Mark's bus driver ran toward us and placed his body in between Mark and me. The police arrived and asked what I wanted to do. I didn't respond right away. I felt like I was

having an out of body experience. Was this really happening to me? "We need to go to the hospital," I numbly responded. The police put Mark in the back of the police car, and I drove separately. As he sat in the hospital room, handcuffed with two guards, the numbness wore off, and my emotions poured like a waterfall.

I felt angry my son had tried to hurt me. I felt heartsick he was handcuffed, because I knew he did not understand what was happening to him. I felt afraid for what this meant for our future. I felt tenderness toward the sweet, innocent little boy inside a man's body. I was scared of him, and yet I wanted to hold him in my arms to save him all at the same time.

When Mark was only a few weeks old, I knew he was different. I took him to a baby group, and while the other moms laid their cooing newborns on blankets, my son screamed. I walked around trying to soothe him, but he continued to cry. As Mark and the other babies grew older, I couldn't help comparing Mark to them.

When he was two years old, we were with the baby group, having some apple pie and ice cream, and one of the little boys said, "Mommy, are we going to have apple pie à la mode?" I was blown away by the difference between the other child and Mark, who only spoke a few words now and then.

We went to the pediatrician, who recommended speech therapy. I had seen an article on autism, and after I showed it to the speech

therapist, she confirmed my suspicions: Mark had autism. With this new diagnosis in hand, I had no idea what it meant for our lives. I began researching and started a home-therapy program with speech, OT (occupational therapy), and ABA (applied behavior analysis). Although he did progress, every time Mark took one step forward, he would take two steps back. I quit my job because no childcare would take him.

Only a matter of months after Joshua was born, I knew he was headed in the same direction as Mark. I would lay him on the blanket, just as the other moms did in baby group, and he would look everywhere but at me. At fourteen months, he was diagnosed with a subtype of autism, PDD-NOS (pervasive developmental disorder not otherwise specified).

By then, we had moved to Idaho, and the state program allowed Joshua to go to an intensive behavioral program for thirty hours a week until he was five years old. We saw huge progress, and I know this program saved my son. He is now thirteen years old, is mainstreamed in school, talks nonstop, and is enthusiastic about the things life has to offer. I often wish there had been an early-intervention program available for Mark where we had lived before.

I joined a parent support group meeting every Wednesday. My husband traveled a lot for business, and this group helped me not feel so alone. I enjoyed having an instant group of friends who understood my life. I knew I wanted to help other parents through a group like this.

After volunteering for years, I became the executive director for Families Together. My favorite event is the Family Enrichment Weekend. We have buddies for the kids with special needs, while the parents listen to educational speakers and connect with each other. There is satisfaction in being able to help those going down the same road. We all have different footsteps, but the path is shared. I love being someone people can talk to, and I cherish the ability to help make things a little better for these families.

After Mark attacked me, I didn't tell anyone about it for over a month. I felt ashamed and sad and scared. Now I talk about it freely because I know others are having similar experiences with their kids. The worst thing we can do is keep it to ourselves and feel alone in our struggles.

The way Mark behaved on that day changed nothing for me. I enjoy his high energy, his happiness when he is outdoors, and riding our tandem bike together. He has some language and is able to communicate more by using his iPad. He is still the same boy I have always loved and will continue to protect and care for forever because he is my son.

Families Together
FamiliesTogether.org

Pamela Lim

Bedok, Singapore

Mary*, Fourteen Years Old, and Joshua*, Thirteen Years Old

Art by Joshua

Growing up in Singapore, excellence was ingrained in me over and over again. In my country, children are held to a high standard of excellence, and anything less is failure. Perfection in grades is expected in the classroom, and perfection in behavior is expected in everyday life. A child is either excellent or ignorant. There is no in between. This has been our culture for almost two hundred years. So when my children were

diagnosed with Asperger's, I was forced to reevaluate everything I was taught as a child.

When my two kids were young, we would pile in the car every Sunday night and head to my in-laws' house for dinner. The kids loved spending this time with their *ye ye* (grandpa) and *nai nai* (grandma) and eating my mother-in-law's special fishball soup with fish dumplings.

We would eat dinner, read, then get the kids ready for bed so if they fell asleep on the way home, we could carry them to bed. One Sunday, we bathed the kids as usual, but when it was time to dry off, I realized I had forgotten Joshua's pajamas. Between his sensory issues and rigid behavior, I knew this was not going to end well. The minute he got any dirt on himself, he immediately washed it off, and the thought of having to put back on his dirty clothes after taking a bath was enough to bring on a full tantrum. My in-laws offered him other clothes, but his rigidity and sensory issues only allowed his mind to singly focus on the clean clothes he wanted. I knew there was no way to change his mind, so to end the tantrum, I went home to get his clothes. To my in-laws, this seemed like weak parenting.

The Asian society is extremely results oriented, which creates a giant roadblock for the different-thinking child. I tried to explain autism to both sets of parents many times, but it is hard for the older generation to understand how a child who doesn't obey or who misbehaves can still be

very smart. They can't see that, occasionally, the right parenting decision is to give in to the demands of the child with autism.

My husband was the first to notice our daughter, Mary, was different than the other kids. In her kindergarten class at church, a poster hung with the title, "How to Know if Your Child Has Autism." He read the poster while waiting for Mary and realized she had many of the traits listed. Concerned, I took her to our pediatrician and told him, "Mary doesn't have eye contact, is very shy, and does not like to socialize."

He replied, "We don't like to give children labels this young. Give it time."

Before I had kids, I was a teacher and loved helping children who were having trouble grasping the concepts. I took the same creativity I used to use with my students to help my daughter get through those first few years of school. But school became more and more difficult, and eventually, even with my help, she could not keep up. She began to feel like a failure because she was not reaching the goals the school set for her, and depression began to set in.

When she was ten years old, I took her to a psychologist, who finally gave her the formal diagnosis of Asperger's. She needed therapy outside of school, but it was so expensive we could not afford it. I decided to go back to school to get my psychology degree so I could understand and help her as much as possible. I fought for accommodations to ease

the demands on Mary at school, and her happiness level increased immensely, as did her grades.

Our son, Joshua, showed more signs of autism as a young child. He had many sensory issues, cried at loud noises, had trouble learning Mandarin, and could not handle schedule changes. He lined up his toys, used self-talk to regulate, and often threw tantrums. It was very tough when he was young to be a part of society. We would have to prepare him when we left the house, warn him of any changes, and be very careful about the timing, or he would melt down. He was diagnosed officially with autism at nine years old, and I used my teaching skills and psychology degree to also help him cope in school and in the community.

After observing how my kids learned and behaved for years, I wanted to use what I knew to help others. I became a special education teacher. So many kids with special needs are bright, but they are not able to perform in the current system of education. I am able to modify the classroom and teaching to meet their needs and use their interests to teach them.

I believe we need to appreciate the small, positive changes a child is making and shift our mind-set to accept ourselves and others as we are right now. All we can do is work on the things we can control. I learn from my own kids and the kids in my class every day. They are so insightful. Imperfection is not failure; it is room to progress.

At fourteen years old, Mary is finally coming out of her shell. She is doing well in school, is in the Young Leadership Program, enjoys fanfiction books, and has a brilliant imagination. She loves animals. She says, "Animals are easier to deal with than people." Mary and Joshua are very close and encourage each other in their autism journey. Joshua is thirteen years old and doing well in school; his speech is flourishing, and he is a gifted artist. Both have been diagnosed as twice-exceptional (meaning they are extremely gifted). I learn so much from my children and all I teach in the classroom. It is a gift to be in their lives.

Autism is lifelong. As parents and teachers, we must be willing to walk alongside our kids, encouraging them to accept and love themselves, so others will love them too. Being proud of our differences and using what we have learned in this life to help others is what I believe to be the highest form of excellence.

Autism Resource Centre (Singapore)

Autism.org.sg

---

* Names have been changed to protect identity.

Judith Ursitti

Boston, Massachusetts, United States of America

Jack, Thirteen Years Old

After dropping my son, Jack, off at the therapy center for the first time, I felt dazed. "Does he really belong here?" I worried. "Am I really a special-needs mom?" I must have looked bewildered, because a group of parents standing in the parking lot immediately reached out to me.

"The first time is the hardest," one parent kindly offered.

"When your son starts to progress, it will all be worth it," another chimed in. They began to share a little about their journeys through autism. Each of their stories had a familiar ring, and I knew, as much

as I didn't want it to be true, I did belong here. As I got in my car and drove away, there was one thing I couldn't shake . . . Two out of the three parents were selling their homes to get more money for therapy.

Along with delivering the news of my son's autism diagnosis, my pediatrician wrote out a very specific prescription for forty hours a week of ABA (applied behavior analysis), OT (occupational therapy), PT (physical therapy), and speech. I took this prescription to the therapy center and enrolled my son. I had great insurance through my husband's company, and it never occurred to me they would not pay for it.

When I arrived home, I called my insurance company to make sure we were covered. I began to explain to my agent, "Because of Jack's autism . . ."

She interrupted me, "Stop! Don't say that word. Never ever say the word *autism*."

"But why?" I questioned. "I am not embarrassed he has autism."

She explained, "Your policy specifically states autism is excluded, so I will pretend I never heard that word. There is no treatment covered for autism."

"Not even speech?" I asked.

"Not even speech," she said. "If he has autism, your out-of-pocket cost will be around five thousand dollars a month."

What did she mean autism was excluded?! Why was autism different than any other disability or health problem? Did insurance companies

think kids with autism were hopeless and too expensive to cover? I felt discriminated against, and I was filled with righteous anger. I was not OK with this injustice.

When Jack was two years old, I knew he was delayed, but I didn't worry. My eldest child was a girl, and I was sure because Jack was a boy he would walk and talk in his own time. On his second birthday, his pediatrician did a developmental screen. Every question she asked, the answer seemed to be no. No, he was not pointing; no, he did not have two-word sentences. In fact, he could only say one word: "ball." As I answered these questions, I reluctantly allowed myself to consider there was something wrong with my son.

We were then sent to a neurologist, who performed the CARS (childhood autism rating scale). Jack scored thirty-nine out of forty. He was severely autistic. Right there in the doctor's office, I sobbed uncontrollably. I was normally so rational and composed, this caught me by compete surprise; my head had been in the sand. I had read all the pregnancy, parenting, and baby books. How did I miss this?

Selfish thoughts ran through my head. *My son is going to be institutionalized. How am I going to handle this burden? How will I be able to have a life?* My husband felt bad for Jack, but I just felt bad for me. People often see how hard parents of special-needs children work and label them "saints." The truth is that we are normal people who just want normal lives. Our responses aren't always right. We are human.

I began reading books, searching on the internet, and connecting with other parents. I got involved with a group of parents working to change the health-insurance laws in the state of Texas, where we lived in 2005. As we fought to have House Bill 1919 passed, I became immersed in the world of autism. I joined with other autism parents to educate myself and fight for our children. The connections and friendships made in this group were my support.

In 2007, HB 1919 passed, requiring insurance companies to cover therapy (including ABA) for children with autism. This was a huge victory!

We moved to Boston with my husband's job. Compared to Texas, the services for a child with autism in Massachusetts were phenomenal! We were offered placement in a private school (paid for by the public school system) where Jack would get one-on-one teaching most of the day.

Because of my work in Texas, Autism Speaks asked me to become their director of state government affairs, and I began traveling all over the United States to help other states duplicate the bill.

When Jack was about eight or nine years old, he wasn't progressing as we'd hoped. We put so much pressure on him to perform, he became aggressive and unhappy. I had to come to terms with the fact that he wasn't going to be one of those miracle kids who comes out of autism. He was going to need help for the rest of his life. I will never give up on

him, but I realized we needed to change our expectations to allow him to be happy and to allow ourselves to enjoy him for who he was. We needed to give him love and support and respect him as an individual.

We began allowing him to learn by doing the things he loved. After school, we started running, swimming, and community outings. His frustration lowered, and his beautiful smile was back.

Jack is now a very tall, handsome boy who loves to run, has abs of steel, and is always on the move. He has about one hundred need-based words and communicates mostly through his iPad. He does not understand safety and still needs full-time help. Of course, I worry about the future, but I have learned to enjoy the day.

Forty-six states now require insurance companies to cover treatment (including ABA) for autism. The insurance companies can no longer discriminate against my child or anyone else's because they have autism. This is my life's work. The best part of my day is when I receive a copy of an EOB (explanation of benefits) from a grateful parent saying, "I can now send my child to therapy." It then sinks in that these bills are affecting real lives around the country, and that is what makes this the most rich, amazing, exhausting journey!

Autism Speaks
AutismSpeaks.org

Leah Seyoum-Tesfa

Irving, Texas, United States of America

Nayab and Yadiel, Nineteen Years Old

I sat in one of the ten brown pleather office chairs surrounding the large, faux-wood table in our school's conference room. Slowly, various teachers, administrators, and district specialists filed in and took seats. They were friendly but guarded, as was I. From past experience, they knew I was a mom who was not only educated but persistent in getting my sons exactly what they needed.

As the principal called the meeting to order, the projector flashed bold print on the screen, saying, "Nayab Tesfa IEP Meeting." Being in

an IEP (individual education plan) meeting meant there was something so wrong with my child a team of experts must figure out how to help him succeed. Being in an IEP meeting meant my child didn't respond to the conventional ways of learning. He did not learn the way my father or my father's father learned. He was different, an anomaly, a puzzle in their eyes.

I sat there with sweaty palms and a fake smile, anxiously waiting to hear the state of my son's progress. Today, it was good news! Nayab was responding well to the therapy in the special communications classroom for children with autism. His language was soaring, and he was motivated to work hard. In fact, he was doing so well they had decided to mainstream him in with typical peers with support for the following year. I let out a sigh of relief and held back tears of joy. Nayab was going to be all right and would be able to function in the world.

Then a second set of paperwork flashed up on the screen: "Yadiel Tesfa IEP Meeting." I was enjoying the victory of Nayab so much that I'd almost forgotten we had another IEP to discuss. As the projector flipped to Yadiel, so did the celebratory mood in the room. No longer was this team of experts looking me in the eye and smiling. Yadiel was not responding to the early-intervention therapy. They still hadn't found a form of communication that worked for him, and he remained nonverbal. He would stay in the communications class indefinitely. The thought of Nayab moving up without his twin brother made my heart

sink. This time, I held back tears of pain. I knew I should be able to separate the two—being happy for Nayab while being sad for Yadiel—but I couldn't. A mother is only as well as her sickest child.

After a difficult pregnancy riddled with complications, my boys were born at thirty-two weeks gestation. They stayed in the NICU for four weeks, and then we brought our tiny, five-pound babies home to make our family of five complete.

At one year old, Nayab began saying some words, but Yadiel would only talk gibberish. By eighteen months old, my gut told me something was not right. At two years old, I asked the pediatrician to do something, but he told me not to worry. My mommy instinct told me otherwise. When the boys were two years and eight months old, I contacted the school district and talked to a speech pathologist, who told me, "It is urgent you seek help immediately, but we can't help the boys until they are three years old."

We started a preverbal speech and behavioral program at the University of Texas at Dallas, and both boys began making progress. As soon as they were three years old, we put them in the communications class through our school district.

The boys could not be more different. Sometimes we would call them "Yes" and "No." Yadiel was always easygoing and happy to go with the flow. Nayab was driven but frustrated and wanted things his way.

From elementary school through high school, Nayab continued to do well. When he went through puberty, however, he became very angry and aggressive and had difficulty self-regulating. We put him on medication, but he would spit it out and say, "Stop poisoning me! It makes me not want to socialize." We found neurofeedback, and within ten sessions, he was a different kid. All his disruptive behavior was gone.

When the therapies continued to be unsuccessful for Yadiel, I took him out of school for a time. I taught him PECS (picture exchange communication system), and he began to communicate. We then switched him over to an iPad so that he could talk with his device. He too became aggressive when puberty hit, but, as usual, the boys would do nothing the same. Yadiel did not respond to neurofeedback.

Within our school district, I noticed there were so many parents who didn't know how to advocate for their children. I would see children worse off than mine getting fewer services, so I started a parent support group to provide them with assistance, education, and resources.

Even though I was helping many families, I felt God telling me I could do more. I am an immigrant from East Africa, and a recent study showed one in thirty-six children of our origin living in the United States has a child with autism. This is almost double the statistic for all the kids in the United States. I knew I could help these immigrant families, because I was one of them.

I started Reaching East African Families with a few local families, and now I am giving assistance to over 170 families across the United States. There is still a stigma bred in East Africa that does not go away when our families move to the States. In our native country, disabilities are associated with a sin of the mother, so no one wants to let others know about their child. Kids are sometimes locked away in private rooms, hidden from the world.

Helping others in this high-need community is my purpose in life. It is a break from my own life and is my way of fighting autism. If I can't beat it with my own children, maybe I can with someone else's. I know I went through this, so I can help others follow where I have already been.

Nayab, now nineteen, has graduated from high school and started college, drives, and works two jobs. Yadiel loves to swim, works at a clothing shop for a few hours a week with a therapist, and still does a lot of therapy. Yadiel will never be as functional as his brother. I have learned to be OK with that. I have one child who has progressed well and one who hasn't. I know the joy and the heartbreak and the love that accompanies both. This only helps me relate to a broader spectrum of families needing my guidance.

Reaching East African Families
ReachFamilies.org

Victor Yermolaev

Saint Petersburg, Russia

Vanya, Twenty Years Old

Talking to Vanya was like talking to a wall. There was no emotional response from him . . . ever. Words cannot describe the longing I felt to connect with him in some way. My love for him was so strong, yet it did not feel reciprocated. Asking what I love about him is like asking what I love about the sun. I am his father, and my world revolves around him. He is my everything.

We knew something was different about Vanya by the time he was one year old. He had no eye contact and swayed back and forth all day

long. A neurologist determined he had a delay in psychological development, but his mom knew it was something more and began to do research on the internet. It was a long process of researching since the internet moved so slowly and the information available online was still very sporadic. She diagnosed him with autism herself before he was two years old.

There were no resources in Russia, no help from the government, and no understanding of autism in the community around us. We had limited knowledge ourselves, and we couldn't find anyone else with a child with autism. No one seemed to recognize the hardship we were going through, and it was difficult because we were so isolated. At times, we were even harassed because of his behavior.

His mom was extremely exhausted because Vanya did not sleep well at night and she was with him all day long without breaks. She was following her intuition to teach him how to communicate, and she began to use pictures to help him learn words. He was able to read before he was able to speak. Every word took so long to learn, but he began to use words to let us know his needs.

When he was four years old, he was finally officially diagnosed with autism by a psychiatrist. We were given medicine, and he started with a speech therapist.

We worked around the clock with Vanya to help him learn. He needed so much help to do any type of normal, everyday activity. We

dressed him, bathed him, fed him, and did everything in between. It seemed he could do nothing on his own. Even though we worked and worked, improvement seemed minimal. Every skill he had was thanks to his mother's hard work, but there was no cure for his autism and no hope of a normal life for him.

Although he was allowed in a preschool, once it was time to go to first grade, no school would accept him. We took him to school after school, but every school told us he wasn't allowed to come back. He didn't cooperate with their inflexible teaching style. Frustrated, he hit a teacher and was eventually labeled "mentally challenged" and "unteachable." We finally found a school that would allow him to attend, but we were his teachers. Although the attitude was better at this school, we still had to teach them how to work with him every step of the way. Eventually, we were so exhausted, we gave up. My wife and I got a divorce, and after Vanya lived with her for a short time, he came to live with me during the week.

Finally, when Vanya was ten years old, we found a website for the Fathers and Sons Foundation. It turned out there were so many other families going through the same thing we were. We just hadn't found them until now. We went to a summer camp for families with autism. This turned everything around for us. As we spent time with these other parents and their autistic children, we began to see what Vanya could be capable of. A glimmer of hope returned. With the proper training, we

would be able to teach him to do everyday things on his own, and it was possible for his need-based language to turn conversational.

While at this summer camp, Vanya and I went hiking together. Finally, we found something we could do together that we both enjoyed. The hiking challenged him in new ways, and something turned on inside him. He began using his inner resources to communicate with us and connect with the world around him. When we got home, everything seemed different. He was doing things differently and saying things differently. And for the first time in his life, I began to feel a nonverbal connection with and a love from Vanya I hadn't felt before. I realized it had always been there, but to feel this from my son was the best thing ever. It is empowering and inspirational to share this very real bond with him.

This new energy enabled me to help others. I became the head of the parent committee at Anton's Right Here Center and poured myself into helping the parents using the techniques I had learned. I remembered how difficult it was when Vanya was young to not have anyone who could share their experience with us. Now I could be the person I wished I'd had at the beginning of autism. I can walk alongside these parents and make sure they don't feel alone or hopeless. It is great to be able to do this for others. Our kids with autism are given to us for a reason: they are our greatest teachers.

Vanya is now twenty years old. He talks with us conversationally, loves computers, plays music, goes to the movies independently, enjoys

socializing with his friends, and reads a lot. He continues to progress every day. He recently graduated from high school, and we are so proud of how far he has come. He was rejected from the vocational training program, so now we are trying to figure out everything all over again. But, this time, we won't give up because we are surrounded and supported by other families living with autism. And this makes all the difference in the world.

Anton's Right Here Center
OutFundSPB.org/wp

Valerie Hu

Washington, DC, United States of America

Matt, Thirty Years Old

When my son, Matt, was in third grade, I was invited to his elementary school for "Circle of Friends" to share with the other students about his condition. Since Matt looked normal, the kids were always surprised when he acted in unexpected ways. When they tried to talk to him, he didn't always answer, and sometimes he would ignore them or say things off topic. This response was confusing, so the school district sent someone in to share with them about autism.

As I sat in the circle with my legs crossed like a third grader, I was encouraged by how much Matt's classmates wanted to help Matt be successful in the classroom. I explained to them how Matt's disability made it difficult to know how to socialize with them. They could help him by talking to him and being patient as he responded. They could also play with him during the free time, and they shouldn't be discouraged if he didn't look like he was having fun. The students were so cute as they sat there wide eyed and full of concentration. Children are beautiful and loving in elementary school; I wished this kindness would last forever. They asked all kinds of questions. One smart little girl was quiet the whole time. I could see the wheels turning inside her head . . . She was working something out. At the very end of our time together, she raised her hand and said, "I know what it is. It is genetics." She nailed it.

I always knew I wanted to be a scientist. I grew up in Hawaii, where it was common to treat medical conditions with herbal medicine. Every time the herbs worked, I was fascinated! I wanted to know the chemistry of those plants and exactly what was making them so effective. So I got my bachelor's degree from the University of Hawaii and a PhD from Caltech, conducted postdoctoral research into membrane biochemistry and immunology at the University of California, Los Angeles, and began work at the George Washington University School of Medicine. Never in my wildest dreams did I expect to be using my

education to work toward figuring out the developmental disability that affected my son.

My son, Matt, was an easy baby. It didn't concern me he walked a little late, but when he wasn't talking by two years old, I began to look into what might be wrong. I took him to a neurologist, who placed some electrodes on his head to check his hearing. His hearing was fine, but the doctor thought the results were consistent with a possible "global communication" issue. That was twenty-eight years ago, and not much was known about autism.

We took him to our school district for further testing. Matt endured six months of testing in a very intimidating environment. I would walk him into the school and place him in a room with six strangers. Then I was required to leave him there alone while they tested him. It was difficult to wait so long to know what was happening with my son, and when we got the results, it didn't get any easier. The experts came up with a diagnosis of PDD-NOS (pervasive developmental disorder not otherwise specified), which is under the autism spectrum.

I immediately went to the library to research this condition and found nothing. There was not even one book, no advice, and no plan to help a child like Matt. It was devastating to get a diagnosis that came with no information about what to do next and no prognosis.

We were given several medications to try, but none of them worked. It made no sense to me to keep shooting in the dark with medications when we didn't understand the biology behind the autism.

We placed Matt in our public school, where occupational and speech therapies were included. He began to make some progress, especially in his speech.

It was tough in the schools because he seemed too high-functioning to be in with the special-needs classes but required the help of an aide in the normal classroom. No one was trained in his condition, and he had behaviors no one seemed to be able to understand. He wasn't aggressive, but when he got frustrated, he would refuse to do what they were asking him to do. They would give him a giant worksheet with forty problems, which was too much for him. He would dig in his heels and not do it. At home, I would take the worksheet, break it down into small, manageable parts, and together we would work to complete the whole worksheet. He could do anything that was asked of him; he just needed it broken down into smaller, more manageable parts than the typical child.

Eventually, he was moved to a special ed classroom with students with ED (emotional disorders). This was not a good mix of kids for him to be around. He was socially unaware, and those kids took advantage of this every chance they got. He was once bitten on the back of the head for no reason at all. Through all of this, we supported him every way

we could, and he continued to make progress despite his educational environment not being perfect.

With another parent, I helped found the Montgomery County Asperger Parent Support Group, a group that worked together specifically to get better education in place for high-functioning teens with autism, PDD-NOS, or Asperger's. The progress was slow, and unfortunately, we did not see the fruit of our labor before Matt graduated from high school.

When Matt got his high school diploma, we were so proud. Now, as a thirty-year-old adult, it is hard to know how much to push him. There is a fine line for learning. He lives at home and navigates all types of public transportation well on his own. He has had the same job since 2008, volunteers at Autism Speaks, and goes to social meet-up groups in hopes of finding a girlfriend.

That smart little girl in Matt's third grade class was right on: since autism runs in the family, it was natural to first look at the genes combined with environmental factors to find the cause. I began taking the same techniques from my previous work and applying them to autism. Not only was the work fascinating, but we were one of the first to break those with autism into subgroups to study so that we can use targeted therapies to treat them with more accuracy.

I love using my scientific knowledge to help those with autism. I was on the original board for Autism Speaks and am on the Scientific

Advisory Board for the US Autism & Asperger Association. The work I have done on autism is more meaningful and rewarding than anything else I have ever done. I am now looking into environmental contributors to autism, and the studies look promising. We will keep searching until we find the cause of the disorder affecting my family and so many others around the world.

US Autism & Asperger Association
USAutism.org

Mai Abo Ahmad

Garden City, Michigan, United States of America
Saif, Fourteen Years Old

I pressed the button to recline my seat, closed my eyes, and attempted to clear my mind. I knew no matter how hard I tried, sleep would not come. The seats on the plane were too close together, and even after twelve hours in the air, the baby on the lap of the woman next to me was still fussing. I had worried unnecessarily for weeks about my son Saif's behavior on the plane. So far, he had been a little angel, barely making a peep.

My mind was still racing from the dinner with my family the night before I left. Every time I thought of my mom and sisters, I wanted to

lock myself in the tiny airplane bathroom and fall apart. Saif and I were leaving the only home we had ever known. My entire family, my support system, was now thousands of miles away in Jordan, and I had no idea when I would see them again. We were moving to the United States of America to get help for Saif.

My husband had left for the United States eight years before to better support our family and to pay for treatments for Saif. For eight long years, we had been apart. I was excited and a little nervous to see him and be a family again. As we walked off the plane, I spotted him, standing there with a dozen roses in his hand, eyes darting through the crowd, trying to find us. He looked older and more handsome than I remembered. Our eyes met, and he ran toward me. Relief rushed over me as he hugged me tight. We had made it to the land of opportunity, and together, we would fix our son.

Saif was a normal baby, hitting all his milestones on time. When he turned one year old, my parents and I noticed some differences. My father thought perhaps he was blind. When that proved incorrect, we thought he couldn't hear. That too proved wrong. We took him to a neurologist in Amman, who did an MRI, genetics tests, and more. Test results suggested he might have autism.

I didn't believe it. I didn't know what autism was, but even when it was explained to me, I was in denial and scared. Time went by, and Saif regressed more and more. His eye contact worsened, and he

began repetitive behaviors. I took him from doctor to doctor, hoping for a diagnosis of anything but autism. I had to come to terms that it was not about me; it was about my son . . . and he desperately needed my help.

After going through a grieving stage, I finally accepted he had autism. I began researching online and found a pediatrician with a child with autism. The pediatrician connected me with a biomedical doctor in the United States. We tried to treat Saif over the internet, but the distance and the cost of importing medicines made it too hard.

Although autism is prevalent in Jordan, no one understood my child. He was always compared to typical children. It was difficult to take him to playgrounds, restaurants, and visits with family, yet I was so proud of my son I took him everywhere. Our families loved Saif but didn't know how to deal with him.

For a long time, I knew I needed to take Saif and join my husband in the United States, but it was so hard to leave my family and everything I knew. When I was completely sure my son would not get better if we stayed, I forced myself to make the move. It was a hard decision, but I had my family's blessing.

My husband drove a truck for a living and rented an apartment for us when we arrived. After picking us up at the airport, we stopped to get blankets and pillows and slept on our apartment floor. This was all we

had to furnish our home for months. My husband was only with us for a short while before he had to go on the road. When he left, I was alone in a country where I didn't know a single soul, did not speak the language, had little money, and could not drive. I was suffocating in my isolation.

The first month was so hard, but it got easier as time went on. With help from a school translator, I enrolled Saif into school and found it was not as easy as I thought to get him the services he needed. We began biomedical treatments to help heal his body, but every way I turned, I had to fight for my son. I was overwhelmed and frustrated. All I wanted was for my son to improve.

I attended classes to learn English and wrote every new word in a notebook. A lady named Roba from the Autism Alliance of Michigan helped me get the correct services for my son in the schools. Saif slowly began to improve. As he made progress, I wanted to help others. With Roba's help, I started the Arab Americans for Autism group to give emotional support to parents whose native tongue was not English. I had learned a lot over the years, and I wanted to share with those who could benefit from what I'd gone through. If I could make their course a little easier, then all the hardship I'd gone through would be worth it.

Saif is now fourteen years old and doing well. He has the most beautiful smile in the world! He is able to talk through an iPad to tell us his wants and needs. Although still quite different from other kids, his amazing personality makes it easy to fall in love with him. There is still

much to do, but we keep going together. I dream about the day we will be able to go back to Jordan to visit my family. They will be so happy to see how much Saif and I have changed for the better!

Autism Alliance of Michigan
AutismAllianceOfMichigan.org

Tania and Kayla Sterchow

New South Wales, Australia

Kayla, Twenty Years Old

Kayla

Growing up as a child with autism in Australia was tough. There was no place for me to go to school, so I was sent to a rough school for kids with mental and behavioral issues.

I walked into the school library one day, dropped my backpack on the floor, and plopped onto one of the many comfortable beanbag chairs. I liked the feeling of my body sinking into the chair and the soft sides curving around my middle, making me feel safe. I liked spending

time in the library. The smell of old books and the quiet ambiance soothed me.

I pulled out my knitting needles and yarn and disappeared into my work. Knitting also soothed me. Each repetitive and predictable movement allowed a worry from the confusing world around me to fade away.

Without warning, I felt an intense pain in the back of my head. My body was slammed forward, and my knitting needles flew across the room. As I tried to pull my body up and turn around, a student was standing over me, kicking me repeatedly in the head until I blacked out.

Tania

I was at work when I got the call from the school and rushed to the hospital to be by my daughter's side. The doctors said she had a concussion and would need time to recover. There were so many emotions going through my mind . . . anger that this had happened, guilt that I hadn't been there, and sadness that my daughter had been treated this way. We spent four days in the hospital before she finally was released.

When the school refused to discipline the student who attacked Kayla, I pulled her out of the school and began a search for a better educational situation.

Some parents and kids are cruel. They don't have the compassion to be kind to someone who is different. When Kayla was younger, we had

parents telling other parents to keep their kids away from her. Because Kayla wasn't like them, they thought she was bad, and I was a bad parent. We got so tired of all the stares and whispers that we bought a farm in the country so we could spend our weekends in peace.

Kayla was sick from birth. She turned blue many times in the first six months of her life, and at fifteen months she had a seizure that almost killed her. She continued to have seizures from that time on. Her behavior was also getting more and more difficult, and she had behaviors that didn't make sense to us. When we were told brain surgery would stop her seizures, we agreed. The seizures stopped, but her problematic behavior intensified.

The doctor's solution was to send us to a behavioral unit to teach us how to be better parents.

Finally, when she was twelve years old, a clinical psychologist observed her at school and diagnosed her with autism.

Kayla

I never fit in at school. I struggle with social cues, and it was hard to make friends. I was never invited to parties. Even though my mum was always by my side, helping me, I was sad when I was a kid. Other kids would play jokes on me. All I have ever wanted was to be like other kids.

After I was kicked in the head and no one did anything about it, I went to a wonderful school, Dapto High Wollemi. For the first time,

people believed in me. My teachers joked around with me and made school fun. Before, everyone was too scared of my autism and the reaction they would get from me. I was allowed to go on school excursions and camps. I learned I could achieve anything as long as I put my mind to it.

I am now twenty years old and in college, and I speak about autism awareness whenever and wherever I can. I want more people to understand autism, and I don't want anyone to experience what I had to. I also volunteer at an autism respite daycare center on Saturdays.

Even though people have doubted me and bullied me all my life, I wanted to prove them wrong. Autism has made me stronger as a result. Autism is a part of me, and even if there were a cure, I wouldn't take it. Autism makes me who I am.

Tania

At one point, when things were particularly low with Kayla, I realized not only did I need support but there were others needing it, too. Autism isolates the family as well as the child with autism. No one needs to go through this alone.

I started a weekly coffee group for parents and grandparents of kids with disabilities. At first, we cried and comforted each other, but soon we were laughing and having fun. In no time at all, we became genuine friends. Because of each other, we are better equipped to fight for our

children and meet their needs. When people are ugly to us, it no longer matters because we aren't alone. I now walk beside many others who understand my life as we make the autism journey together.

I love that after everything she has been through, Kayla never gives up. My father was always very supportive; one of the last things he told me before he died was, "I have great faith in Kayla. She will be OK." And he was right!

Autism Unit, Wollemi, Dapto High School
Web2.Dapto-H.Schools.NSW.edu.au/tag/wollemi/

Katherine Alvarez

Miami, Florida, United States of America
Joshua, Thirteen Years Old

I watched from the window as Josh pulled up in front of my parents' home. He stepped out of the car and walked up the sidewalk wearing light-colored blue jeans and my favorite black, collared shirt. I remembered loving how the dark color made his tan skin glow and his brown eyes shine. When we first met, I stared at him for hours, learning every detail of his face, as he made me laugh until my stomach hurt. But now even the sight of him repulsed me. I had no desire to go to our favorite Mexican restaurant. Even with

a margarita to dull the ache, I didn't want to be anywhere near him. When we said our "I dos" eleven years ago, I had never imagined it would be possible to feel this way about the man I was once so madly in love with. I'd never imagined I would no longer want to call him my husband.

Josh rang the doorbell, and as I greeted him, the scent of his cologne brought up a gag reflex in the back of my throat. I turned my head to the side to avoid his scent, and we politely said our hellos. Every syllable I pronounced was flat, lacking any real emotion. We were separated but trying to make it work. The discomfort we both felt made it clear we were just going through the motions until one of us was brave enough to say it was over. Autism had slowly sucked the life out of me. I had no love and no energy left for anyone else but my son. Eighty percent of marriages with special-needs kids end in divorce, so I knew it would take a miracle to save ours.

When my son, Joshua, was around a year old, he did some odd things, causing my mommy instinct to be on high alert. He started to withdraw from us, quit pointing, and stopped answering when we called his name. I worried he had hearing issues, but when I put an Elmo DVD on across the house, he would come running. When police sirens blared loudly nearby, he wouldn't react; instead, he would sit with this glazed look on his face. The hollowness in his eyes was the most heartbreaking part. Where had my son gone?

My godson was diagnosed with autism, and I began to attend appointments with his mom. All the information they were sharing with her seemed to apply to Joshua too. When Joshua started lining up toys, there was no doubt in my mind. I knew he would join my godson with a diagnosis of autism.

We went to a well-known neurologist with high hopes he would be able to give us some direction. The doctor barely said hello when he walked in. He whipped a string out of his pocket and held it in front of my son's face. When my son didn't respond, he bluntly said, "That's autism," scribbled something down on the file, and walked out the door. No advice. No help. Just a formal diagnosis of Autism Spectrum Disorder 299.00 (F84.0). Joshua was two years and three months old. It was Cinco de Mayo, and it was the worst day of my life.

I became a hot mess. I couldn't sleep, I couldn't eat, and I became obsessed with figuring out how to help my son. I read some information on ABA (applied behavior analysis) and found a study by Dr. Ivar Lovaas stating 47 percent of the kids who did his treatment plan of forty hours a week for two to six years became indistinguishable from their typical peers. I knew this was the answer.

We were living in Miami and had no insurance coverage and no way to afford bringing help to us. So we uprooted our little family and moved to Las Vegas, where Joshua could attend the Lovaas Center for Behavioral Intervention at a more affordable rate. We left our entire

extended family. My husband quit the job he had been at for over ten years, and we headed west to heal our son.

We moved into a small, two-bedroom apartment, and six months later, by the time my husband finally found a new job, the isolation had begun to set in. I was desperate to connect with other moms, so I started going to TACA (Talk About Curing Autism) parent meetings. I loved the support and mutual sharing of information. My son was progressing and making great strides in language and behavior, but he began to have medical issues—constipation and insomnia. He cried a lot and seemed to be in pain. TACA moms helped me address those issues one by one and shared resources about DAN (Defeat Autism Now) doctors, who also helped get to the bottom of his pain. Those women brought me hope. I knew as soon as we moved back to Miami I would open a TACA chapter and begin helping others, just as those ladies had helped me. Life is easier when you do it together.

After four years in Las Vegas, my marriage was a mess. We decided to pack it up and head home to Miami. We lost our house, declared bankruptcy, and moved in with my parents. We continued spending every dime we had to treat my son. I could not stop until he was better. My every waking moment was occupied with autism. My husband and I had no alone time, and within a few months, we separated.

Around the same time, we decided to join a church. Immediately, the church jumped in to support our broken family. They prayed for us

and encouraged us to keep trying to put our marriage back together. We went to a FamilyLife retreat, and it was there I began to fall in love with my husband all over again. We learned how to put God at the center of our marriage. We learned what real, selfless love was and how to give each other grace. I feel blessed to experience falling in love with my husband for the second time.

I don't celebrate autism, but in our lives, it taught us lessons we didn't even know we needed to learn. It has given me the ability to help other autism parents in Miami the way I was helped in Las Vegas. Our son is now thirteen years old, and he is happy, hardworking, and motivated to learn. He is a fighter, and I wish I had his strength and determination. He still has plenty of struggles, and I will continue to fight for him, but not at the expense of my marriage. My husband is an amazing father; the love he has for our son is captivating and beautiful. I am so glad we are in this together.

TACA: Talk About Curing Autism
TACANow.org
2017ff.TACANow.org/katherine-alvarez

Indrani Basu

New Delhi, India

Nano, Twenty-Four Years Old

I stood outside the pub, not quite sure what to do with myself for the next few hours. I wasn't welcome inside, but I couldn't take my eyes off the front door . . . not even for a second. Cars and people were bustling by, and there was nowhere to sit and wait. I took a seat on the curb, pulled out my phone, and vacillated on whether I should post this on Facebook.

For the last eighteen years, all I had ever wanted was for my son, Nano, to become independent. I knew all the extra schooling, therapy,

and life-skills training he'd endured were leading up to a moment like this. It was his eighteenth birthday, and like any young adult, Nano wanted to celebrate. Since he and I did everything together, we'd made plans to go out that evening. But as he walked in the door of the pub, he'd turned to me, said firmly, "No, Mama, no, Mama," and shut the door in my face!

At first, I was bewildered, but then a sense of pride swept over me. My son had asserted his independence, and I wasn't going to stand in his way. I would wait for him outside to make sure he didn't wander out into the street when he was through celebrating. As odd as it may sound, being shunned by my own teenage son made me feel a little more normal.

Nano is my only child, so when he didn't develop speech by two years old, I wasn't overly alarmed. I adored him and his quirky personality; we were inseparable. When he was three years old, we joined a play group, and I was shocked to see how different he was from the other kids. I decided to talk to my doctor and was told, "You are a young, overanxious mother. He is fine."

A feeling something was not right with my son remained, so I requested more tests. We did an MRI, a CT scan, and a hearing test. All were normal. My instinct told me to keep digging.

At four years and three months, Nano was given a diagnosis of PDD-NOS (pervasive developmental disorder not otherwise specified)

from a doctor in Bangalore. I was encouraged by this because I was convinced that if we did two years of intense therapy, he would be OK, and our lives would be back on track. There were not a lot of options for kids with autism in the late 1990s in India, but we were able to find a place with a watered-down version of ABA (applied behavior analysis).

Two years later, Nano wasn't making the progress I had hoped. I had been so sure we would be able to fix his disability in two years, but autism was not cooperating with my timeline. I struggled to accept this new reality and grieved for my son . . . and for our lives together.

We went through some rough years during puberty. His behavior was extremely challenging: he had lots of anxiety and regressed. We were not getting the services we needed, and I knew we had to find a better situation for him.

A remarkable lady named Merry from Action for Autism came to our area to give a talk about autism. It was life-changing for me. I realized for the first time there was nothing wrong with Nano; he was just different. I stopped trying to fix him and began to love him exactly as he was. I asked Merry if he could go to Action for Autism's Open Door School. In six short weeks, he made huge progress. The school accepted him for who he was, used lots of visuals and social stories, and took the noes out of teaching, adding in reinforcers instead. A positive environment is so important for our kids. They can feel if someone cares

about them. Soon Nano stopped hitting, started listening to us, and was happier than ever.

Finally, we had a good plan to help him, and having a plan gave me the hope I needed to move forward in my life. I started volunteering at Action for Autism to benefit my son, but I soon grew to love the difference I was making in others' lives, too. I took over the parent-child training, in which I helped parents work with their own children. Seeing the intimate interaction when the children began to respond to their parents and the joy it brought the moms and dads was invigorating. Helping these families became my lifeline. I feel exceptionally lucky to do what I do. It is hugely satisfying to see the transformation in these families.

Nano is now twenty-four years old, and we take him everywhere. In India, there is still a stigma with special-needs people, but I have noticed our attitude toward our son often translates to others. We set the tone for how they should treat him.

He is a happy young man with a twinkle in his eye. He loves food, listens to retro music, and works at the vocational center at Action for Autism, using his fine motor skills to make jewelry. He has need-based language and uses two-word phrases. We have learned it is important to celebrate the small things. The other day, his grandma was struggling to open an oil jar, and he walked up to her, took the jar, opened it, and handed it back to her. That was huge for us!

I have learned to value autism for what it is. My son is lovely to hang around, and I am happy to spend every day with him . . . even if it means hearing, "No, Mama!" once in a while!

Action for Autism
Autism-India.org

Laura Kasbar

Spokane, Washington

Ana and Max, Twenty-Two Years Old

I sat down on my bed and let out a gentle sigh. Maybe for one tiny moment I would allow myself to relish the quiet of my bedroom away from the kids. I felt my eyelids getting heavy, and just as they began to close, my brain snapped back on, and my eyes popped open with alarm. *Wait!* I thought: *Why isn't anyone pulling on my leg, crying, or asking me for a snack? Why is it so peaceful in my home?* Instead of taking advantage of my moment to relax, I had to get to the bottom of this odd silence. I was sure the kids were into something they shouldn't be.

As I peered around the corner from the hall to our living room, I did a double take. All five of my kids were sitting close together on the couch staring at the TV. My three-year-old son, Max, who had severe autism, looked indistinguishable from the others in this setting. I smiled at the thought of him someday being able to truly hang out with the other kids, and then my heart sank as I remembered that after six months of forty hours a week of one-on-one ABA (applied behavior analysis) therapy, Max still did not have the ability to say even one single word.

The only time Max appeared engaged was when he was watching TV. He would even laugh at the funny cartoon humor and hide behind a pillow when there was a scary part. He would interact more appropriately with the movie than he ever had with us. When he wasn't in front of the screen, he was wandering around our house, lining up everything possible and avoiding all human interaction.

Watching my son paying such close attention to the TV, I had a thought. I'd gone to the University of France, and, as an adult, I learned four languages. I still have trouble understanding French if I cannot see the lips of the person speaking. This gave me an idea. Max never looked at us. He never saw our mouths actually move. Maybe if we figured out a way to make him watch our mouths, he would be able to talk. Since he was so attentive to the TV, I made a video to teach him the difference between the words "Barney" (a figure from his favorite TV show) and "cup." I videoed my mouth saying "Barney" five times with a Barney

figure next to it, then I did the same thing with "cup." The next day, Max said his very first word: "Puc." He mixed up the *c* and the *p*, but it was the most beautiful word I ever heard! I was on to something with this video-mouth thing.

Because I had three older kids, when my twins, Max and Ana, were born, I already knew how babyhood was supposed to go. When the twins weren't talking right away, I didn't stress . . . Each kid was on their own unique schedule. After all, my husband talked late and walked on his toes, and he turned out fine. But when Ana began babbling and showing intense frustration as she tried to communicate, I knew something was off. She would roll back and forth across the floor of our living room, screaming. She would also pick a toy at the beginning of the day, grip it tightly, and refuse to let go of it all day long. Max, on the other hand, was easygoing. He made no sounds, had no eye contact, and had no interaction.

I understand how parents are clueless, because I was. Even with all these red flags, autism never crossed my mind. I knew about autism, but it never dawned on me that my kids, Ana and Max, could have it. While I was in the hospital having my sixth child, the twins were evaluated by the school district. As soon as I was out of the hospital, they wanted to meet with both me and my husband together.

As I walked slowly into the school, still sore from childbirth, with a four-day-old baby in my arms, I expected to be meeting with one or two

teachers. Instead, we walked into a room with a large conference table filled with teachers, psychologists, and behavioral and speech therapists. I knew by the looks on their faces something was very wrong, but instead of telling us, they kept asking us questions. "Tell me more about Max?" they would say. "How does he behave at home?"

After going back and forth like this for quite a while, one of the experts finally said, "No talking is indicative of autistic behavior."

Someone else went on to say, "Ana has intent to communicate. She should progress well, but Max is so severe he will likely need to be institutionalized."

I had a nervous breakdown. I couldn't sleep. I couldn't remember anything. I cried all night. But somehow, I knew I had to push through. Those experts telling me Max belonged in an institution was the best thing they could have said to me. It drove me into action. As parents, we need to have a very healthy combination of fear and hope to move forward. If we don't have hope, we stop, and if we don't have fear, we don't bother. I had plenty of fear, and I was determined to find hope.

My husband and I got on the internet and began researching. The only proven therapy for a child with autism at that time was the Lovaas applied behavior analysis, and this therapy required at least forty hours a week. We also found the Individuals with Disabilities Act (IDEA), which said if the school diagnosed my children, they were required to provide the therapy to help them. It was starting to make sense why the

school hadn't wanted to tell us right away the twins had autism, but even so, I had now found hope.

The school worked well with us to come up with creative solutions to get the therapy for both the twins. Ana responded right away to the therapy, but after six months, Max still had no response . . . until the day I tried the homemade video. After Max said "puc," I made more and more videos to teach him. My husband stayed up many nights to make videos of me mouthing words with objects. In just a few weeks, Max had learned over thirty words and was continuing to add new words every day. By the time he was eight, he had caught up to his peers.

I was so excited about what was happening in my home, I started sharing this video system with others. The videos caught on, and word spread even more. It was wonderful to experience the joy of the parents when they heard the first word come out of their child's mouth. Through Skype and Google, I traveled around the world at no charge, helping other families learn how to do this for their own children.

We created a web-based platform, Gemiini Systems. Research on Gemiini has been published by professors from several universities. We were able to keep costs low and set up scholarships for families who couldn't afford the system. The system is currently helping thousands of families in over twenty countries.

Both Ana and Max now enjoy typical lives like any other twenty-two-year-olds. They graduated high school at sixteen years old (partly

homeschooled) and have already completed several years of college. Ana has tons of friends, loves to sew, and is super creative. Max works at a grocery store, traveled to France for school, and loves foreign languages.

The most unexpected gift in this journey is that instead of me taking care of Max for his entire life, he already takes care of me. He is willing to help me all the time with his little brother and makes my life easier every day. As an extra added benefit, he even engages with us now more than the TV.

KultureCity
KultureCity.org/lovewithoutwords/gemiini

Lotta Lagerholm

Malmö, Sweden

Anton, Eighteen Years Old

As we readied ourselves to return home to Sweden, my son, Anton, began excitedly repeating the words, "Airplane. Yes, please. Airplane. Yes. Please." Very rarely does Anton talk spontaneously, but when he does, his words always have something to do with vacation. Even though the plane rides and changes in scenery are difficult for him, we prepare him well, and he has grown to love his time away from home with our family.

The difference between Anton successfully completing a "normal" activity or melting down in utter frustration is planning. Out of necessity,

I plan everything we do down to the smallest detail. Then I make a book with pictures explaining to him exactly what we are doing, so he can understand and predict the situation we are about to put him in. The only problem is this does not leave room for the unexpected. And so much of everyday life is responding to the unexpected.

In planning our flights, I take into account when Anton will be hungry and when his moods will be the most balanced. I have a bag packed with activities and snacks to keep him occupied, make sure we can board early, and book him a window seat. I always book the seat directly in front of him for his sister, so no one is bothered if he kicks. Plus, I inform the airline of his autism. Having to think ten steps ahead is exhausting, but this is what I must do for our family to vacation.

We boarded the plane early, as planned; then all the other passengers, along with their different faces, smells, and movements, streamed past us to take their seats. In an effort to keep Anton from becoming overstimulated, I encouraged him to look out the window at the workers repetitively putting the baggage on the plane. I knew this predictability would calm him and set us up for success.

Unfortunately, during this particular vacation, when it was time to take off, we waited and waited on the tarmac. The time between getting on the plane and taking off is the hardest for Anton. Waiting five minutes feels like waiting five hours. The longer we waited, the more he became agitated and started screaming. Since he was fourteen years old, his cries

were loud and alarming, and people began to feel uncomfortable and ask questions. We asked the flight attendant to let others know about his autism and to politely ask for their patience. But the flight attendants began pressuring me to make him calm down, and the added stress only made him spiral down further.

The captain came out of the cockpit and said, "Ma'am, can you guarantee your son will calm down after takeoff?"

"I can't guarantee anything," I responded, "but he normally calms down soon after we get in the air." After takeoff, we were in the air fewer than five minutes before the captain turned the plane around. Despite the fact that Anton was completely calm by the time we landed, we were still asked to get off the plane.

It took us thirteen horrendous hours to get home, when it should have taken three. Anton was noticeably upset about the incident for at least six months and hasn't said, "Airplane, yes, please," since.

As a toddler, Anton didn't speak much. His doctor told me this was normal because he was a boy and we spoke two languages in our home. I knew nothing about autism and did not suspect anything was wrong. When he was three years old, we had a new pediatrician, who was very knowledgeable and diagnosed him with autism.

Learning I had a child with autism was like falling into a cold, black, precipitous hole. There was no end, and as I fell deep and deeper, I couldn't see a way out. I cried hysterically. *What will happen when my*

child grows up? How can I support and help him when life is so demanding and there are so many lifelong problems? What will become of my life? How will his siblings handle this stress? How can I do everything for all of them? I thought I was going to break into a million pieces.

I tried to research online and learn about his condition, but every time I read something, it was too painful. This disability affected every part of the child, and the need was lifelong. Now, every time I looked at my child, all I saw was the autism. I was filled with guilt. Why did I feel so sad for my child, whom I love? What could I have done differently for him not to have autism?

We began ABA (applied behavior analysis), which not only helped his behavior but helped me to understand his behavior always had meaning. Because he couldn't talk, I needed to look at what had happened right before he acted out to realize what he was trying to tell me with his behavior. We also used the TEACCH (Treatment and Education of Autistic and Related Communication Handicapped Children) method and began speech therapy, sensory integration, and the Listening Program. He started to speak some words to get his needs met.

I volunteered at the Autism and Asperger Association Skåne, and eventually, they chose me to be on the board. I traveled around Skåne to schools and preschools and held lectures to spread autism awareness. It is very rewarding to share with interested teachers how it's easier for children to succeed in the classroom if their teachers understand autism.

I also was on a team that produced internet-based training for parents whose zero- to six-year-old child was newly diagnosed with autism. I am currently working on a project, Antons Hus, in which families with autism can come and enjoy a stress-free vacation. No one should have to go through the horror of getting kicked off a plane.

It took years, but I finally realized I was never actually grieving Anton. He is the same child he was before his diagnosis. He works hard daily to communicate and uses his creativity to get his needs and wants met. I had been grieving the life I'd wished for him. I had to come to terms with the fact that the life we were living was different, not worse. I now see the world from a different perspective and actively seek creative solutions in this unexpected direction our lives took. As it turns out, even people without autism have trouble responding to the unexpected.

Antons Hus

AntonsHus.se

Amanda Shannon

Wheat Ridge, Colorado, United States of America

Lily, Eleven Years Old

As we had every evening for the last month, my four-year-old daughter, Lily, and I walked into the garage we had converted into a therapy room. We grabbed her favorite Dr. Seuss book, *Green Eggs and Ham*, and therapy supplies and climbed into the hyperbaric oxygen chamber for two hours of treatment. The soft chamber was a large, blue tube big enough for two people to sit in comfortably.

We had a comfortable routine now. First, we did therapy targeting her language skills for an hour, and then Lily chose some activities we

could do together. After getting past the claustrophobic feeling of being trapped in a small space, I had grown to enjoy this time of bonding with my daughter, who was normally always on the move. Autism steals the connection between mother and child, so being able to hold her in my arms for a solid two hours made me feel the closeness I had been craving since the moment she disappeared into her own world.

Autism had caused her eyes to glaze over. Even if I was standing right in front of her, I could not reach her. I wanted to know her. I wanted to know what she was thinking, what she was feeling, and her likes and dislikes. I wondered if she loved me as much as I loved her, or was I irrelevant in the world she lived in inside her head?

By the time our two hours was up, Lily had fallen sound asleep. I quietly unzipped the chamber, scooped her up, cradled her like a baby, and stepped out of the chamber. Her eyes fluttered open for a moment. She looked straight into my eyes and quietly said, "I love you, Mommy." Tears streamed down my face as I drank in the most beautiful four words I had ever heard. Finally hearing those four words from Lily made every dime spent, every relationship severed, every tear cried, and every dream put on hold 150 percent worth it.

As a baby and young toddler, Lily had a series of ear infections, was late reaching her milestones, was rigid about having to hold two things (one in each hand) at all times, didn't cry, only had a few words, and would sit still in one spot for a long period of time. As if those weren't enough red

flags, at two years and eight months old, she rapidly began to spiral deep into autism. She started drooling, babbled to the sky, giggled nonstop, lost all eye contact and language, and no longer responded to questions.

At two years and ten months, she was diagnosed with mild-to-moderate autism. The doctor told us she would never speak and that there was only one proven therapy, which was called ABA (applied behavior analysis). Even with that therapy, she would likely not progress much, and then we would have to institutionalize her.

That prognosis was unacceptable to me. I knew there had to be other ways to help Lily. I researched online and found other therapies that seemed to be helping kids with autism. We moved across the country from Florida to Colorado for better treatment options. I hired therapists and ran a comprehensive program consisting of ABA, speech, occupational therapy, neurotherapy, and more out of my home. I began to take what I already knew about nutrition and integrative medicine and collaborated with like-minded doctors to treat Lily. She had inflammation, so we treated her with hyperbaric treatments; we did IVIG (intravenous immunoglobulin) to strengthen her immune system; and we treated the heavy metals naturally. Treating each physical issue her body had was helping enormously. We worked eighty hours a week!

She began to talk at four years old and was potty trained at seven years old; her OCD (obsessive-compulsive disorder) lessened, her eye contact improved, and she began to follow what we asked her to do.

I opened a wellness center to help other kids like Lily, but I soon realized there were many who could not afford these treatments since nothing was covered by insurance. That is when we started the Lily Grace Foundation, which provides children and families diagnosed with autism spectrum disorders with education, resources, research, and scholarships for medical and integrative therapies. We also put together "relaxation stations" within the public schools to provide a sensory break for those who need it. We added yoga and meditation to help kids learn to self-regulate. We offer respite and other types of parent support. We are collaborating with the University of Colorado to do research.

My work is as therapeutic for me as it is for the people I help. Helping families going through similar situations helps us all to go through the grieving process together.

No matter how verbal a child is, how capable they are, or how aware they appear to be, they are seeing and hearing everything going on around them. We need to talk positively, build them up, and find ways to empower them by allowing them to use their gifts. The foundation has not only allowed me to give back to the community around me but allowed Lily to help with this.

At eleven years old, she already uses her gifts to teach yoga classes. She has a wonderful sense of humor, loves nature and animals, and is very sweet. It has been a joy to see her come out of the autism haze

and develop this enchanting personality. With Lily, there is no negative; everything is beautiful. And we could all use a little more love in the world today.

Lily Grace Foundation
LilyGraceFoundation.org

Amit and Saar Wolfman

Ashdod, Israel

Saar, Twenty-Four Years Old

Amit

My son, Saar, has a voice, and what he has to say is important. He may be different, but he feels the same feelings we all feel. Despite what others may think, even people with autism have their feelings hurt when someone treats them as unimportant or ignores them as if they were not even there.

When Saar was a teenager, I was on a never-ending quest to help him become self-sufficient and often encouraged him to try new things

by himself. On one occasion, we walked into a pizza restaurant in Tel Aviv, and I gave him twenty shekels to buy pizza and a drink. I told him to walk to the counter and politely order while I waited for him a short distance away. He waited patiently in line, and when it was his turn, he said, "One slice of cheese pizza and one grapefruit juice, please." The restaurant owner ignored him and went on to the next person. When the owner was free again, my son repeated, "One slice of cheese pizza and one grapefruit juice, please." Again, the owner acted as if my son didn't exist and went on to the next person.

After this happened three more times, the owner looked at me across the room and shouted, "What's for you, ma'am?"

By this time, my blood was boiling, but I managed to keep my cool as I walked to the counter. "My son has told you several times what he would like," I responded.

But the owner replied angrily, "This is no school, and I have no time for you to teach your kid what to say. I am not wasting my time, so if you want something—you tell me." I looked at my son—his brown eyes wide with innocence and his hand still stretched out with the money—and my heart broke. I choked back tears as we quickly walked out of the restaurant. Saar had done everything right, and although he couldn't verbalize it, I knew the manager's cruelty had affected him.

In the first year of his life, Saar developed normally. He walked, smiled, and laughed on time. His only issue was he wouldn't eat solid

foods. At one year and ten months, I took him to a routine checkup with the doctor to discuss his feeding issues, and the doctor blurted out, "Madam, it seems to me your son is autistic." I thought she was insane, and I booked several other appointments to prove that diagnosis wrong. I was stunned when Saar finally was given the formal diagnosis of PDD-NOS (pervasive developmental disorder not otherwise specified), a subtype of autism.

My entire world crumbled down around me. In shock, I immediately blamed myself. What had I done wrong to make him this way? Did I not eat healthily enough during my pregnancy? Maybe I hadn't moved around gently enough when he was in my belly, and this caused the damage? Or was it just my bad genes? I was angry at everyone and everything. I was angry at God, at fate, at the doctors, and at the paramedical team. I felt so powerless to help him.

I did not know another soul with a child with autism, and my loneliness was unbearable. There was no internet like there is today and no support anywhere. The only information I found was two outdated books about autism in Hebrew.

After continuing my search, I came across the Israeli Society for Autistic Children (ALUT), which was a great help to me. Eventually, I went through the grieving process and started to accept the situation. We put Saar in occupational, speech, music, and hydro therapies and saw slow glimpses of progress. He began to talk and follow directions.

This made me realize I had some control in his outcome. I dug deep down inside myself and began to really fight for my son. I fought and won, getting him in the very best kindergarten around. Year by year, skill by skill, he continued to gain abilities and is now doing quite well.

I did not want another mother to ever experience the traumatic loneliness I felt after my son's diagnosis. Together with some other autism parents, we asked ALUT to establish a hotline. This hotline enables a parent with a new diagnosis to call and talk with a real person who truly understands, because they, too, have heard those devastating words, "Your child has autism." On our "Parents for Other Parents" line, we listen, give advice, and help the parent get involved in the community. This open line has been going strong for over fifteen years and has helped thousands of parents begin their autism journey with confidence and hope.

Saar is now twenty-four years old and quite successful. He paints, plays the piano, is a photographer and a marathoner, and is training for his first triathlon. He also volunteers in the Israeli Air Force. Most importantly, he has learned to be an advocate for himself. This journey has been not only mine but his too, and what he has to say about his life is just as relevant.

Saar

Like many other boys my age, I like to play football and ride a bicycle. I also like to play the piano, paint, and hang out with my friends. I love

listening to classical music, operas, and Hebrew songs. I don't watch the TV program *Big Brother* because they just talk all the time, and it bores me, but I never miss the programs *Israeli Idol* and *Dancing with the Stars*.

Sometimes when I look at people, they make strange movements with their faces, and I do not understand what that means. I can't tell when someone is sad or happy or scared or excited, and I don't always know what acceptable behavior is. I try to remember how to behave correctly, but sometimes I forget. Occasionally, I hear a sound that really hurts my ears, and I have to put my hands over my ears to stop the pain. I try hard to understand people I don't know because their voices sound a bit different from what I am used to. When people look me in the eye, it confuses me, and I lose my concentration and stop listening to what they are saying. I know I am a little different, but each one of us is a little different than the other.

The Israeli Society for Autistic Children (ALUT)

ALUTFriends.org

Dawn Neufeld

Frisco, Texas, United States of America
Will, Twelve Years Old

Photo Credit: David S. Irvin

In American football, the tight end is a versatile position who has a dual role on the offensive side of the ball. He is tasked with blocking for the running back, but his fame, fortune, and fantasy football stats come from catching the ball. He is primarily known for receiving passes from the quarterback over the middle of the gridiron. This middle of the field is a dangerous area . . . dangerous to the team because a turnover can happen easily and dangerous to the player because it can be hazardous to his health. Many times, just as he

turns in anticipation of catching a pass, the other team will take him down. But like any seasoned football player, no matter how much pain the hit causes, the tight end gets back up, joins the huddle, and waits for the next play . . . knowing the same thing could happen to him again.

My husband, Ryan, was a tight end for the NFL's Buffalo Bills when our son, Will, was born. Little did I know that what Ryan was experiencing on the football field was preparing us for the fight of our life when Will was diagnosed with autism.

Will was a perfect baby. He hit all his milestones. When he was about thirteen months, I started to notice him behaving differently than other toddlers his age. He seemed extra sensitive to lights and sounds and would tense up and begin to cry when exposed. At our Gymboree Mommy & Me class, he refused to participate in the circle time, instead opting to go down the same slide over and over for the entire hour. At a football banquet, he screamed bloody murder, as if in pain, every time people applauded. When Sundays came, football games were even worse; the loud noise and the bright lights bothered Will, so we had to leave him home with a sitter.

For us, football wasn't just a game, it was a lifestyle. When I was pregnant, I couldn't wait to sit on the sidelines with my son in the players' wives' section, cheering on my husband with the other families.

It grieved me that I couldn't bring Will to the games and share this experience I loved so much. My idyllic football-family dream was fading fast.

At eighteen months, we had Will evaluated and began speech therapy, occupational therapy, and physical therapy. At three years old, he was diagnosed with autism. We were crushed by the hits we were taking in the "middle field" of life. Our world came crashing down along with all the hopes and dreams that we had envisioned for our family. We were devastated.

The first person I reached out to was my friend Holly Robinson Peete. She had been very vocal about her son with autism, and I knew she would be able to encourage me and walk me through what to do. I also read Jenny McCarthy's book *Mother Warriors* and felt hope for the first time since Will's diagnosis. I learned Will would make progress if we were persistent. My motto is "this too shall pass," and I realized it was no longer about the limits our child had but about how I could help him reach his full potential. Autism was not a death sentence for our hopes and dreams. Learning to appreciate the world from a different perspective changed everything.

Because I had always been active in charity work, it was natural for me to take what I learned through my son and help those also facing autism. Ryan and I became involved with Autism Speaks and the Autism Treatment Center. We began speaking at autism conferences and events,

and I used my platform as a competitor in Mrs. Texas America to raise autism awareness. As I told CultureMap Dallas, families dealing with autism are my heroes:

> We're all just an adversity away from needing a hand up . . . Volunteering reminds me to count my blessings and not take anything for granted. . . .
>
> Until you've had to live with autism 24 hours a day, seven days a week, 365 days of the year, it's hard to explain how traumatic it can be for families. My son is the greatest gift in my life, and he makes me smile every day, but his autism has literally brought me to tears at times. I truly admire families who are trying to put the pieces of this puzzle together.[3]

Will is now twelve years old, and because we picked ourselves back up, worked past the pain, and joined the huddle over and over again, he has made great progress. As he progressed, he was able to come with me and enjoy Ryan's football games. Now Will is verbal, quite mischievous, and has the funniest sense of humor. We watch *The Voice* TV show every week; I love that we can enjoy this together. Will has taught us to manage our expectations and appreciate the smaller things in life.

Ryan created the football program for Miracle League, a sports program designed specifically for children with special needs. We watch

Will carry on the football legacy on his special-needs team. Our family is enjoying a slightly different football-family dream than we imagined, but it is absolutely just as rewarding!

Autism Treatment Center
ATCOfTexas.org

---

3. Diana Oates, "The Litigating, Philanthropic TV Host and Supermom on Living in the Moment," CultureMap Dallas, November 27, 2013, http://dallas.culturemap.com/news/society/11-27-13-dawn-neufeld-the-broadcast-autism-influential.

Riitta Nykänen

Turku, Finland

Matias, Twenty-Three Years Old

Another tough evening, and I was beyond exhausted. My baby had finally fallen asleep around 10:00 p.m. after I had rocked her for over an hour. According to the clock, I had put my head down on the pillow only a few hours ago when a loud noise jolted me out of a deep sleep. As I sat straight up in bed, my heart racing, it took me a minute to remember where I was and another to realize my four-year-old son with autism, Matias, was already up for the day. It was only one in the morning! After doing this for months, the words "sleep deprived" did not even begin to describe my condition.

I dragged myself out of bed, made sure he wasn't in immediate danger, and started a pot of coffee. It would likely take two pots to get me through another day. Matias used to have trouble falling asleep but had switched to falling asleep quickly and waking up in the middle of the night ready to start the day. I did everything I could think of to help him sleep through the night. We walked for hours, put him to bed at different times, took sugar out of his diet, bought blackout curtains, and had him jump for hours on the trampoline. Nothing seemed to change his sleep pattern.

Most mornings, he would wake up between 1:00 and 3:00 a.m. with abundant energy that never seemed to fade. We watched him every second he was awake to keep him safe. He got into everything inside our home and showed no understanding of what might be dangerous. This alone was exhausting during the day, but during the night, it was unbearable. My mind had become permanently hazy and my emotions out of check. I wanted to think about something else besides autism, anything else, but autism had taken over my life.

When Matias was two and a half years old, he still had no words. We took him for a medical checkup, and he was placed on a wait list for speech therapy. Once he received speech, he gained about five words, and then all those words disappeared. Two weeks before his fourth birthday, a neuropsychologist diagnosed him with autism. I didn't know anything about autism, and I felt very helpless. The moment I received his diagnosis, my mind went through his whole life and how different

it would be from the life I'd envisioned for him. I was completely overwhelmed, sad, and unsure how to cope with the news. I broke down for a few days, but I knew I had to get back up and figure it out.

In Finland, we have great health care, and a path was immediately laid out for me to help my son. He was placed in a special daycare program with four children and four adults (one teacher and three assistants) per group. He received speech therapy and occupational therapy, and they used the TEACCH Method (Treatment and Education of Autistic and Related Communication Handicapped Children). This daycare was brilliant with my son, and we didn't have to pay extra because he had special needs. He then transitioned to public school using the same therapies and structure. He remained in the public school system, with excellent services, until he was sixteen.

When he was still at the daycare, we heard about a natural sleeping aid called melatonin. We gave it to Matias in hopes it might help him sleep, and he immediately slept through the night. Having more rest changed our lives dramatically. I now had the patience and strength to deal with the demands of autism on a daily basis, and for the first time in many months, I was able to have a positive outlook. We began to enjoy Matias and his quirky personality.

Since speech did not seem to be possible, we found other ways to help him communicate. He understood pictures and used them to tell us what he needed. He learned to type with a keyboard and eventually

to talk using an iPad. This made me realize that kids with autism understand what we are saying even when they are unable to respond with words. It is so important to speak positively in front of them, because if they overhear and misinterpret what we say, they have no way to ask for clarification. It is unhealthy for them to internalize so much of what they hear.

Matias is severely autistic and will always require help. When he was seventeen, there was an opening in a well-respected group home near our house. It was a tough decision, but we decided to move him. For the first time in almost two decades, I had the time and energy to think about something besides autism. And strangely enough, one new hobby I chose was helping other families with autism.

When my son was young, I wondered where all the parents were who had already raised kids with autism. It seemed such a waste of knowledge to go through all of this and then disappear. I wanted everything I'd gone through with my son to matter, and I knew I could share what I had learned to help others.

I was asked to talk to some autism parents at my son's old school. The parents were so touched by my son's story that some were in tears by the time I finished. There is peace in actually meeting a person who has made it through the worst autism has to offer and knowing there is light at the end of the tunnel. The power of peer support removes the isolation and allows us to move forward.

Later, I was asked to talk to some parents at our local autism association's peer support group. A few years after that, I joined in a program set up by the Finnish Association for Autism and Asperger's Syndrome. In this program, I was trained to support families with a new diagnosis and encourage them to join local peer support groups.

In addition to encouraging new parents, I translate materials for our organization. I also started writing a column to share the weird and wonderful aspects of autism and how those on the spectrum relate to our world.

My son comes home every other weekend, and we spend time doing all the things he loves. We bake his favorite pies, play memory games, and take long walks. Although he still doesn't talk, I know he understands what we are saying. He is quite charming, loves slapstick humor, and is happy in life.

Even though I spent a long time wishing autism wasn't in my life, I know I wouldn't be able to help others the way I do without living it myself. Seeing other parents confidently going through autism and helping them feel strong is brilliant! I feel so grateful to be able to play a part in their lives because of what I learned with my son.

Turun seudun autismi- ja ADHD-yhdistys Aisti ry
AistiYhdistys.fi

Yetta Myrick

Washington, DC, United States of America
Aiden, Thirteen Years Old

My blood pressure began to soar, and I could feel my heart about to burst through my chest. I took a long, deep breath in and slowly let it out, attempting to control my anger. Then I punched in the numbers on my cell phone and called Channel 5 News. Someone needed to shine a light on what was happening to these kids with autism, including my son.

My son, Aiden, was four years old on the first day of summer school. For most kids, summer meant sleeping in, staying in pajamas all day

long, playing outside with friends, and begging Mom to go for ice cream when the sun peaked midafternoon.

But for Aiden, summer meant a transition to a new schedule that brought on all kinds of stress and anxiety. He thrived on the predictability of the school schedule. If he could do the same thing at the same time each day, it helped him cope with all the other unpredictable activities that didn't make sense to him. It was always difficult for him to transition from the safety of a familiar routine, so we decided to extend the school year into the summer. The school and teachers would change, but once he was there for a few days, he would begin to feel comfortable with the new schedule.

Thankfully, on this first day of summer school, I did not have to work and was able to drive Aiden to school. Walking in with him, I tried to diffuse his anxiety by saying I would stay until he was settled. When we arrived at the office, I asked, "What classroom will my son be in?"

"I am not sure," responded the receptionist. "There are some kids with autism in the cafeteria."

I walked down the hall and followed the echoes until I found the cafeteria. Several kids with autism were jumping up and down, flapping their arms, talking in gibberish, and running wildly around the cafeteria. One child had his hands over his ears since the noise was so loud. "Where is my son's classroom?" I asked the teacher. "He is very anxious

to start his new routine." Her answer is what caused my blood pressure to rise.

"We don't have a classroom or any supplies for these kids. No one seems to know what to do with them. We have been unable to get help from the administration of the school."

A school that was unprepared for kids who relied on a schedule and had high transition anxiety was unacceptable. Each child in the cafeteria was someone's son or daughter, and each of them deserved the chance to succeed. If this was happening on the very first day, I can only imagine what would have gone on with no parents present.

I grabbed crayons and a few odds and ends out of my car to help entertain the kids in the cafeteria. At the end of the day, the camera crew from Channel 5 met me at my car. My son climbed in the back seat and instantly fell asleep. The newsperson began, "Aiden is not exhausted from learning but from doing nothing all day long . . ."

At three years old, Aiden still was not talking. I took him to the school district for an evaluation and then to the neurologist, who gave us the formal diagnosis of autism. I wasn't sad and didn't mourn the child I'd thought he would be; instead, I took a different approach. He has a disability, and that is hard, but I will always choose to look at his strengths and provide him with as much support necessary to help him be successful. My driving force as a single mother was and always will be to get him the help he needs.

Autism for me was baptism by fire. I jumped right in with both feet to begin fighting to get him all the services he needed from the public school district. I couldn't afford to pay for private therapy, and I was already living with my parents, so I prepared for the fight of my life. The schools are required to give him a free and appropriate education, but that was not happening. Since the school could not provide what Aiden needed to learn, I hired an education advocate, and we sued the district for nonpublic placement. Only then was Aiden able to go to school in an appropriate environment using the things he enjoyed to learn.

I was never upset my son had autism, but I was furious it was so difficult to get him the services he needed. I knew as an educated professional that if I had trouble navigating the system, then others would need guidance as well. I started the DC Autism Parents support group to share what I had learned with other parents. When parents come together, there is power in numbers, and with numbers, we can create change. If everyone does a little bit, it goes a long way.

After meeting so many moms and dads who were mentally, emotionally, and financially drained by autism, I also started the DC Autism Buddies program. This program lets parents drop their kids off and have a much-needed night out.

Aiden is now thirteen years old. He is easygoing and willing to try new things, and he loves classical music, art, and swimming. I take great pains every day to remove the "mommy blinders" and really see

his deficits so I can help him. We work on those deficits by using his strengths. It might take two years for him to learn a skill, but he is capable, and he will learn it. I am teaching and engaging him in everything we do together.

All any mom wants is for her child to be happy. This shouldn't be different because my son has a disability. I keep this in the forefront of my mind as I am raising Aiden and living my own life. If it takes suing a school district or calling the Channel 5 News, then I will do that and more to give my child the best chance at a happy life.

DC Autism Parents
DCAutismParents.org

Magdalena Kukulska

Zielona Góra, Poland

Tobiasz, Eight Years Old

I know it sounds weird, but sometimes I wish there were a physical marker for autism so people would know right away that my son, Tobi, is different. Tobi is a handsome boy with dark, chocolate-brown hair and sky-blue eyes who looks the same as any typical child his age. So when his behavior is not what people are expecting, we are often subjected to harsh criticism from those around us. If it were possible for people to look at him and realize right away he has special needs, maybe they would be a little kinder.

When Tobi was six years old, we took him for ice cream. He loves numbers and math, so we always work on this everywhere we go. As we walked up to the ice cream trailer, I began quizzing him: "One scoop of ice cream costs two zloty, so if we get two scoops, how much will it cost?" For no known reason, instead of answering a question he normally enjoys, he started screaming.

Before I could calm him down, a man got in his face and yelled, "What's wrong with you?! You need to get out of here!" The man was so aggressive that I could not just stand there and watch him scream at my son.

"Shut up!" I yelled back. "He has autism. What is your excuse for being so rude?" The man became quiet and walked away. I felt bad for the whole situation; we never know what is going on in the lives of the people standing next to us.

Tobi was a typical baby. He talked and waved goodbye. But as he got older, he began losing skills. He stopped using language to get his needs met. Instead, he would walk in the kitchen, plop down on the floor, and start screaming. Somehow I was supposed to know this meant he wanted something to eat. The guessing became excruciating. Then he stopped eating most foods, screamed even more, and began counting everything. When he was two and a half years old, I took him to our general practitioner, who mentioned he thought Tobi might have autism. I felt grateful for the guidance, so I took him to Dalej Razem, where he was formally diagnosed.

At first, I was so upset, I couldn't even look at my son. We would go to the park, and instead of sliding down the slide with the other children, he would sit by himself playing with the sand the entire time. I didn't know why this was happening to us. By this time, I was a single mother, and I felt all alone.

I put him in a typical preschool, but he was kicked out. They told me, "This school is only for healthy kids."

"Then why do you have a child with Down syndrome?" I inquired.

"Because children with Down syndrome are lovable," they replied without any regard for my feelings. This was the most hurtful thing anyone had ever said to me. Tobi is so lovable. He was just misunderstood.

Thankfully, I found a new school for kids with autism that integrated them with typical peers. It was very expensive, but he received five hours of therapy within the school day and was seen regularly by a psychologist. The classroom ratio was three teachers for every four kids. They also had a parent support group that helped me connect with other parents, and I began to feel less alone. After only two weeks of this school, I saw progress in Tobi. Little by little, step by step, he began to use his words to communicate. Instead of only saying no to everything, he began to say yes when he wanted something we offered. He started to add to the foods he would eat. The first time he ate fish, tears of joy streamed down my face.

My brother, who is a sports therapist, introduced me to exercising with kettlebells. I looked forward to getting away from thinking about autism and putting my energy into doing something for myself. The first time I lifted sixty kilos, I was ecstatic! I realized if I could lift this much, then I could do anything! My depression started to lift, and I married a long-time friend who loves my son as his own. It is so important for me as an autism mom to take time for myself. It isn't selfish to be away from my family for a short time; it actually helps me be a better mom to my son.

My brother then came up with the idea of doing a fundraiser for autism using kettlebells. I called it "Million Swings to Autism." This idea quickly became a national movement in which people all across Poland joined in to swing kettlebells for autism.

People kept congratulating me and saying what a big deal this event was, but I was just doing my part to raise awareness of autism. I wanted to help and will continue to help keep this event going each year.

Tobi is now eight years old. He is highly intelligent and reveals his gifts with counting, numbers, and dates. He will look at a bowl of cereal and tell me, "Twenty-five cereals." Somehow he knows without even counting. He is fascinated by animals and insects, especially grasshoppers, and tells us all about their lives. He also loves to swim and play with superheroes.

I take Tobi everywhere with me so he can learn. If we don't take the time to show our children with autism what they need to know to be in our world, they are never going to figure out how to fit in. I don't expect him to be perfectly behaved, and we are learning how to respond to those who react unkindly when he isn't. I hope someday everyone will be aware of the challenges of autism and show compassion.

Stowarzyszenie Pomocy Osobom Autystycznym 'Dalej Razem'
DalejRazem.pl

Sharon Manner

Madison, New Jersey

Kerri, Twenty-Six Years Old

Photo Credit: Jade Yoga Mats

Having been a yoga teacher for more than thirty years, my greatest desire is to help others experience the same satisfaction and happiness I feel. The use of breathing techniques and natural healing has allowed me to live in health and peace for as long as I can remember. So when my daughter, Kerri, was going through a difficult puberty, I am not sure why I ignored my instinct and allowed her to be admitted to a psychiatric ward.

When Kerri was thirteen years old, she began experiencing severe gastrointestinal problems and hormonal imbalance. Instead of relying on what I knew best, natural healing, I took her to a highly esteemed doctor at one of the most prestigious university hospitals in the country. He ran multiple tests and then gave me his grim professional opinion: "Your daughter has a dual diagnosis of autism and schizophrenia, is violent, and needs to be admitted immediately." I was in shock. A thousand thoughts raced through my mind. Kerri had never shown signs of violence, and although she was going through a difficult time, schizophrenia did not seem right. But he was the expert and was educated in these types of illnesses. Despite my hesitation, I agreed.

Since children with autism had to be admitted to the psychiatric ward, I allowed her to be admitted upon the condition she would have her own room. She was only thirteen, and I worried about her safety and what she might be exposed to. A few weeks went by, and Kerri was slipping away. She was on seven different medications and looked sicker than ever. "We believe her condition will be helped with shock therapy," explained the doctor at our next meeting.

"Shock therapy for stomach problems?!" I said in horror. "I am taking her out of this hospital *now!*"

Red flags had been everywhere. How had I not seen them? What was going on at that hospital was not in my child's best interests, and my fears were confirmed five years later when her doctor published a study

on the effects of shock treatment on girls ages thirteen to fifteen with a dual diagnosis, including autism. I was appalled! My daughter would have been a guinea pig for her doctor's study!

When Kerri was born, I knew immediately she was different. She had this heightened consciousness and was aware of everything around her. She was startled by even the smallest noise, only used peripheral vision, and needed to wear headphones to drown out the sounds invading her world.

At two and a half, we took her to a neurologist, who diagnosed her with autism and urged us to do as much as possible to help her while she was still young. I was devastated. I made appointments with many specialists over the next six months to find help, causing us both great stress and anxiety.

Not long after her third birthday, I had an epiphany while watching Kerri happily playing in the pool with her siblings. She was laughing and smiling and having fun. From that day on, I decided that as long as she was happy, that was all I cared about. I didn't need to make her into the perceived version of "normal"; she would be her own "normal." I would encourage what she was good at and allow her to be the best, happiest version of herself.

In my search to find a school supporting my vision for Kerri's life, I went through ten schools before I found one teaching with compassion and love and using the children's own gifts to help them

succeed. Kerri thrived in this environment and finally began talking at eight years old. She stayed at this school all the way through high school.

After her doctor suggested shock therapy and I pulled Kerri out of the hospital, I went back to my roots with natural medicine. I gathered all the experts I knew in alternative medicine and formed a team to get Kerri well. We slowly weaned her off all the medications except one and treated each symptom by finding the root cause. We integrated yoga poses and breathing specifically formulated to calm the nervous system, aid in digestion, and encourage good sleep. Kerri's health greatly improved, and her happiness returned.

One day, as we were driving to school, she opened the window and threw her headphones out of the car! That was her way of telling me she no longer needed them. For the first time in her life, she was able to handle the hustle and bustle of the busy world around her! She was calm, regulated, and empowered. I smiled and told her how proud I was of her for taking such a brave step in her life.

Together with the specialists who helped Kerri get well, I formed Ashrams for Autism. We created a healthy environment for parents to pursue treatment together with their kids through yoga practice and holistic medicine. We teach the "why" behind everything we do, so no parent will ever be put in a situation where they go against what they think is the best treatment for their child. We also offer stress-management

programs for the parents of kids with autism to help them cope and see a silver lining in autism.

At twenty-six, Kerri is thoughtful toward others, plays the piano like an angel, and has a sweet, innocent relationship with her boyfriend. Our children are the result of the environments we allow them to be in. I am filled with gratitude for all the loving teachers, therapists, and practitioners who surrounded Kerri with love, kindness, and encouragement, enabling her to grow up to be the divine, beautiful young woman she was destined to be.

Ashrams for Autism
Ashrams4Autism.org

Maria Kaminski

Osnabrück, Germany

Daniel, Forty-One Years Old

Even something as simple as cooking dinner was nearly impossible because my son, Daniel, needed to be watched every minute of every day. It had only been a few seconds since I took my eyes off of him to work on the meal, and he was already banging his head as hard as he could against the wall over and over again. I ran to him, grabbed him, and took him into my arms. My body replaced the wall as he thrashed his head back and forth. This was painful, but at least I was protecting him from incurring brain damage from hitting the hard surface of the wall.

Daniel began hurting himself shortly after he turned two years old. At night, we moved his bed away from the walls, and I put mittens on his hands so he wouldn't tear at his skin and pull his fingernails out. During the day, I tried to keep him as busy as possible with physical activities such as horseback riding and swimming. It broke my heart to not know what was wrong with my child. He had no language to tell me what was hurting him or why he wanted to harm himself. I felt so helpless. All I could do was watch him vigilantly and protect him as best I could.

When Daniel was a baby, he wasn't responsive at all. He had no voice, did not look us in the eye, and refused to allow anyone to touch him. We began speech therapy when he was nine months old, and he was diagnosed with Kanner's Autism when he was two and a half years old.

It was 1978, and no one knew much about autism. But though I may have a handicapped child, I am not a handicapped mother. After doing research at the library and talking with Kanner therapists, I knew there was so much I could do for my son and others. There was no place for my son to get help, so my husband and I put an announcement in the newspaper to find like-minded parents with autistic children.

Once we found other parents who were also desperately trying to help their own children, we pulled together to raise money for a therapeutic center for autistic children and sued the government to pay for the therapy. The goal of our center was to be caring and considerate of our children while educating them. We fought to get autistic children

supported within the schools and within the workplace and then to receive the help required to allow them to live independent lives. I am proud of what we have been able to accomplish as a team.

Because of Daniel's aggressive and self-aggressive behavior, we felt very isolated at times. Although we were supported by our families and therapists, finding other autism families in the same situation was crucial in pulling us out of our isolation.

I had no time to worry about my feelings of having a child with autism because I was so busy setting up the center to get Daniel and the other children the help they needed. I knew we only had a few years of early intervention before Daniel would need to be ready for school. In addition to speech, Daniel received daily behavioral therapy. Our goal was to integrate him with his peers. Daniel was one of our success stories! Through our therapeutic center and years of therapy, he was able to attend the special school and graduate with his peers.

Today, Daniel talks (a lot!) and is a self-confident man who lives his own life within the community. I help him get dressed every day, and then he goes to a sheltered workshop (a respite program which offers fun activities). He sails with an inclusive group, goes horseback riding, plays sports, enjoys classical music, and visits pubs and disco clubs with an assistant.

His favorite time of the year is when we go on a hiking trip with other autistic adults, because it always turns into a special experience. In

Austria, we learned to use cable cars to get up the mountain. In Lisbon, the German ambassador invited us to a private barbecue in his garden. In Scotland, we stayed in a giant hotel that looked like a castle. As we walked in, Daniel blurted out, "Look! What a wonderful group home!" I love how straightforward he is. I know he means exactly what he says.

One day, he said to me, "Mama, you are mine heart!" This was a beautiful confirmation of what I'd already felt: he really did love me, and our deep relationship was real to both of us.

It is OK Daniel has autism because he can still have a quality life as long as we take care of him with dignity. Watching Daniel experience happiness and live a full, active life makes me grateful for my autism team and makes every bit of extra work we put in over the years worth it.

Autismus Deutschland e.V.

Autismus.de

Donna Levey

San Francisco, California, USA

Dolan, Eleven Years Old

As the school bus headed home, I slouched down on the seat and enjoyed my last few minutes of freedom. I knew the minute I walked in the door, the full care of my brother, Bobby, would be on me. At only eleven years old, I had become his primary caregiver.

Bobby was the youngest of us four kids, and he was completely fine as a baby. But after his first birthday, he began having seizures, stopped talking, played with a piece of string for hours, and rocked back and forth all day long. My parents were devastated and completely shut

down. When he was four years old, the doctor diagnosed him with severe autism and bluntly told my parents, "Your kid is retarded." They couldn't handle what Bobby had become, and as the eldest, I was now responsible for him. I would wake him up in the morning, change his diaper, dress him, feed him, and get him off to school. After school, I was responsible for watching him at all times, changing his diapers, feeding him, bathing him, and putting him to bed. Even on the weekends and summers, I didn't get a break.

I loved my brother with all my heart, but he was too much to handle. Often, the family would go out to a barbecue or a gathering with friends, but I was told, "Not you, Donna. You stay and take care of Bobby." When I was in eighth grade, I worked up the nerve to tell my parents I wanted to go live with a relative. Instead, they decided to put Bobby in a state mental hospital, where he was placed in a wing called the "Vegetable Ward" for children age five and under. The year was 1962.

In this joyless ward, there were naked babies with their arms and legs tied to their cribs, crying all day long. I felt so sad for these kids, and every time I visited Bobby, I promised myself I would someday adopt and save two kids from the system.

I grew up, got married, and began working as a special education teacher. Because I was never able to save my brother, I felt compelled to help special-needs kids. My husband and I had two healthy children of our own, but adopting two more was never far from my mind. The

adoption laws in the 1970s would not allow a working mom to adopt, so we waited.

After my own kids were grown and the adoption laws changed, I began fostering Dolan when he was four days old. His biological mother had been on crack, so I knew it would be an uphill battle. The beginning was brutal to watch. He would tighten up into a ball because of the pain of withdrawal, cried all the time, and couldn't handle being cuddled. He came out of his drug haze around seven months and then began showing signs of autism. I was worried I was crazy or imagining it because of what I'd gone through with my brother. Dolan had food-texture issues, walked on his toes, was obsessive, startled easily, and had sensory issues. Human Services knew something was wrong and were frantically trying to get him adopted while he was still little and cute and before they had to disclose a diagnosis. I was not going to let some unknowing parents adopt a child they didn't know had issues. What if they weren't prepared for a special-needs child, or worse, what if they shut down and didn't care for him, just like my parents? I couldn't let this happen to Dolan. I had fallen in love with him, so I adopted him. By this time, I was fifty-eight years old.

On Dolan's second day of preschool, the psychologist met me at the door after school. "Your son is scaring the teachers and students," he stated. "He is telling us he sees angels flying through the classroom and hears babies screaming from the ceiling." I requested test after test, and

finally, Dolan was diagnosed with autism, along with additional labels of emotional disturbance and psychosis. I pulled him from preschool and found a wonderful school that nurtured and supported him. He had a rough beginning, but loving him was the key to helping him flourish.

When he is doing well, he can be a lot of fun. He is an incredible artist and has many friends. I adopted another little boy who was a year younger than Dolan. His mother was also addicted to crack. Dylan came out of the drug haze at four months and is able to function normally. I loved being able to give Dolan a brother, and they became very close.

I am very involved at Support for Families of Children with Disabilities. We do movie nights, family nights out, and parent support. I am a parent mentor and attend IEP (individual education plan) meetings to make sure kids are getting the services they need in our public school system.

I tried really hard to work with the system to get Dolan all the help he needed. At one point, he became violent, and I asked for mental health support. Instead of giving the support as promised, CPS (Child Protective Services) took him away. There was no abuse or neglect, but because I am a senior citizen, they thought I couldn't handle him. He was ripped away from his home, his wonderful school, his friends and family, and everything he knew. I was devastated.

At sixty-eight, I still have a lot of energy, and I am using that energy to get him back. I joined PACC (Parents Against CPS Corruption) to

fight for children's rights, and I help parents who have been wronged by CPS.

I thought I would be retired and living in Hawaii by now, but life often takes us in a different direction than we planned. We can't always control what happens to us, but we can choose to use the energy it brings in positive ways to help others. I plan to use the negative feelings about what has happened to keep fighting for my son and to help others fight for their children.

Support for Families of Children with Disabilities
SupportForFamilies.org

Josh and Megan Harris

Maui, Hawaii, United States of America

Gage, Fourteen Years Old

Megan

It was early in the morning, and I sat all alone on the couch in my boyfriend Josh's living room. We had only been dating a little while, and although I knew about his son, Gage, we had never met. A bushy-brown-haired little child with shiny brown eyes peeked around the corner. He clutched his *Finding Nemo* stuffed fish tight as he sauntered in a winding path toward the couch. He sat down at the furthest end of the couch and awkwardly scooted closer to me. He could not keep his

body still. There was no language and no eye contact. He sat right next to me and then leaned back into the cushions. As we rested there in silence, I felt a connection with him that didn't quite make sense. I knew he could feel it too. Somehow we were meant to be together.

As I watched Josh treat Gage with care and compassion, I could see Josh was kind and loving and had all the traits of someone I wanted to spend the rest of my life with.

Josh

Even though Gage had trouble walking and struggled with balance at an early age, his speech was crystal clear, and he was alert. After he turned two, he began to have seizures, lost his language and eye contact, and began to talk gibberish all day long. I walked into the Children's Hospital for help with the seizures and left with an autism diagnosis. In an instant, I had become a single dad with a two-and-a-half-year-old with autism.

Gage's behavior became more unpredictable. He was having meltdowns every hour, hitting, and head butting. I knew I needed to connect with others who had walked down this road before me. I began dedicating myself to online research, went to conferences, and placed Gage in occupational, speech, and behavioral therapy.

One day, I took Gage to play at the park, and within minutes of trying to be active, both of us were physically exhausted. Younger

kids were running circles around us, causing a lightbulb to go off in my head. We needed to change our physical health to heal his mental health.

When I met Megan, it was as if the world around me stopped. All I could see were her eyes. We were both in other relationships, so the timing was not right. Gage's birth mom was in and out of his life, and once our divorce was final, Megan and I began to see each other. She had never dated someone with a child, but I could see how good she was with him, how much she cared, and how connected they were from the very first time they met. I proposed to her on New Year's Eve; I knew that together, there was nothing we could not accomplish.

Megan

Once Gage's birth mom relinquished her rights, I adopted Gage as my own son. Even though I already felt like his mom, it was wonderful to make it official. I began taking Gage to all his therapy appointments. It was fascinating to see the impact these therapists were having on the kids by playing with them while targeting learning. I couldn't stop thinking about all the kids like Gage I could help, so I went back to school to become a speech therapist.

As a speech therapist, I noticed most of the kids with autism had behaviors impeding their ability to learn. I then went to school to become a BCBA (board certified behavior analyst). With the combination of

these two degrees, my ability to help kids with autism was endless. Not only could I help the kids who were my clients in a more efficient way but I was able to share my knowledge with the other moms to help their kids. I poured myself into educating these moms, and it felt so good to be able to share what I learned because of my son.

Josh

We did a complete overhaul on our lifestyle, including our diet. No more junk food or late nights with little sleep; whole-body health was now top priority. We went on a strict, whole-food diet, with Gage also gluten-free. We added in vigorous daily exercise. I quit my job as an IT consultant and became a fitness and personal trainer. We began down a completely different path of natural treatment, allowing our bodies and minds to feel a million times better.

At times, it was hard for our family and friends to understand the changes we were making, but almost immediately, Gage's asthma and allergies improved. Soon, he slept through the night, and the bags under his eyes disappeared. He began to make great strides in his other therapies, so there was no doubt in my mind we were on the right track.

Us

As we looked around us, we could see so many kids with disabilities suffering with unhealthy lifestyles. Modern-day sports are so orga-

nized and competitive there is no place for special-needs kids in these environments. Special-needs kids need to be taught how to actively play using things they already enjoy. We decided to combine our new knowledge in whole-body health and exercise with behavioral and speech therapy to start a program called Autism Dynamics. We planned fun, appropriate activities, and just like no two kids are alike, no two programs were alike. Each child had an innovative and creative individualized plan to help him reach his health goals. In addition to exercise, we used speech and behavioral therapy to work on social and teamwork goals.

It was so rewarding to be able to give back to other families with what we learned from Gage. The kids we worked with were helping us as much as we were helping them. We are now embarking on a new adventure in Maui to fully embrace our healthy lifestyle. We have found yet another need to fill: providing special-needs families with respite while they are on vacation. Giving families the ability to drop off their special-needs child in a safe environment while on vacation makes the vacation more enjoyable for everyone. While we have these kids, they will not be sitting around watching TV and playing video games. We will be working with them toward their health goals.

Gage is now fourteen years old, is extremely healthy, talks up a storm, and is very social. He will have a happy, productive life. He loves being active every day with us and his little brother and sister. Our road was

not without bumps and difficulties, but each evening, as our family sits on the beach watching the sunset through the brilliant colors in the sky, we are reminded that it still remains true that as long we are together, we can accomplish anything!

Imua Family Services
ImuaFamilyServices.org

Luciana Arantes

Patrocínio, Brazil

Gabriel and Rafael, Six Years Old

In living with autism, attitude is everything! It is a daily, sometimes hourly, choice to minimize the negative and focus on the positive. If I didn't choose to see the good in our life, I would never leave the house, because my twin boys tend to get us into some pretty sticky situations.

My boys, Gabriel and Rafael, won't sit still for an entire meal . . . ever. On the special occasion when we do go out to eat, we always choose a place with a playground or some type of entertainment. This

allows them to play awhile, eat their food, and then play some more. It isn't the most relaxing evening out, but this is where we are at in our lives, so we make the best of it.

On one such night, my husband and I walked into the restaurant, each tightly holding one of the boys' hands. The boys are prone to wandering, so we always keep them close and never let them out of eyesight. We gently pushed through the crowd to the hostess stand to give our name. While waiting, we took advantage of the playground, and once we were at our table, we ordered quickly. When I handed the waiter back the menus, I noticed the boys' seats were empty!

I didn't need to look far because they had made themselves a little too comfortable at the table next to us. Gabriel was sipping on a lady's juice, thankfully using his own straw, while Rafael was helping himself to her main course, grabbing the meat from her plate with his hands.

I tried not to overreact. The bigger picture was that this wasn't the first time this type of thing had happened, nor would it be the last. It is important for the boys' social development to keep taking them out into the community. I sighed with relief when I realized the stranger was showing my boys grace. "Help yourself," she said with a smile. "Aren't you boys cute?!" I apologized profusely and thanked her for her kindness. As my husband pulled the boys back to our table, we talked a little more, and there was one less stranger in the world.

As an architect, I love to plan and design. Often I will begin designing a building in my head, but as it comes to life on paper, it takes on a completely different direction. Life is like that, too. My boys were developing normally until they were about one year old. My plan for our family was still intact. At a well visit, our pediatrician noticed they were not speaking as expected, so she referred us to a phonoaudiologist.

A few months later, before they were even eighteen months old, they were both diagnosed with autism. That was the day my plans and dreams for my family took a different direction. I quit my job to stay at home and devote myself to helping my boys.

We live in a small town where not many resources are available. My husband and I traveled with the boys to other cities to seek treatment. We started neurocognitive therapy, Floortime therapy, sensory integration, speech therapy, and some other alternative treatments. The boys began to slowly make progress. We saw a light turn on as they understood and responded to requests and looked us in the eye.

I traveled almost every weekend to participate in workshops about autism and enrolled in courses to get my pedagogy (education) degree. This information gave me knowledge and methods to better teach Gabriel and Rafael. My husband took on more work to pay the extra expenses. Instead of wallowing in how hard it was, we chose

to believe we were on a mission. I knew our dedication would bring many rewards.

In Brazil, when you receive an autism diagnosis, there is no government help. We were paying for 100 percent of the boys' care out of our pocket. Kids with autism weren't even guaranteed a public school education until a law was passed in 2016. When the nonprofit Municipal Center of Specialized Educational Service opened in my town, I knew part of my mission was to volunteer.

I shared everything I'd learned in my course work with other parents. I helped with therapy sessions, participated in case discussions, and loaned out the teaching materials I designed for my boys. I created an online group for parents and professionals to share knowledge. I love empowering other parents to be able to help their own children. Every case of autism is so different, and I learn from them as much as they learn from me.

Gabriel and Rafael are only six years old, but they already have made great progress. They are very affectionate and see the world in a carefree and simple way.

This new direction in my life taught me what really matters. It is good to have plans and dreams, but not everything is in our control. Perfection isn't possible, but learning from our mistakes is. I have learned we are all equal, despite our differences, and to take things slowly because everything has a time and a reason. I no longer worry

about the small things and have more patience. Every little achievement is celebrated and appreciated. Most importantly, I learned we are to love and help others using what we have gone through. Pouring ourselves into others transforms lives . . . especially our own!

The Municipal Center of Specialized Educational Service
cmaee@Patrocinio.mg.gov.br

About the Author

Photo Credit: Pala Photography

When her daughter, Lizzie, was diagnosed with autism at the age of two, Julie Hornok jumped into researching and implementing a thirty-hours-a-week home-therapy program. This program treated Lizzie's behavior and speech, along with diet and medical interventions to heal her body. A few years later, as her daughter made good progress, Julie went through her videos and began a video blog (LizzieHornok.Blogspot.com) showing Lizzie's progress to encourage others.

As a result of the video blog, Julie became the go-to mom for helping parents with a new autism diagnosis and was honored to accept a position on the board of the National Autism Association of North Texas. She was also asked to blog for AutismSpot. Blogging regularly enabled her to encourage and help thousands across the globe through humorous, heartfelt stories about Lizzie and videos showing the therapies she was using to help her daughter progress.

Through AutismSpot, Julie discovered her love for writing. She has published short stories in multiple *Chicken Soup for the Soul* books and received an honorable mention in the memoirs / personal essay category of the eighty-sixth *Writer's Digest* Annual Writing Competition in 2017. Her work has also appeared in *Parenting Special Needs Magazine*, *Autism Parenting Magazine*, AutismSpot, *Thrive* magazine, *Literary Mama*, and many more.

Julie is passionate about supporting families with autism and lives in Texas with her husband and three children. Connect with her at JulieHornok.com.

Join the *United in Autism* worldwide community at Facebook.com/juliehornokunitedinautism.